MIX
Papier aus verantwortungsvollen Quellen
Paper from responsible sources
FSC® C105338

Kathrin Kalcheva

Whistleblowing and the NZA case

Managing change and Human Resources

Anchor Academic
Publishing

Kalcheva, Kathrin: Whistleblowing and the NZA case. Managing change and Human Resources, Hamburg, Anchor Academic Publishing 2016

Buch-ISBN: 978-3-95489-493-2
PDF-eBook-ISBN: 978-3-95489-993-7
Druck/Herstellung: Anchor Academic Publishing, Hamburg, 2016

Bibliografische Information der Deutschen Nationalbibliothek:
Die Deutsche Nationalbibliothek verzeichnet diese Publikation in der Deutschen Nationalbibliografie; detaillierte bibliografische Daten sind im Internet über http://dnb.d-nb.de abrufbar.

Bibliographical Information of the German National Library:
The German National Library lists this publication in the German National Bibliography. Detailed bibliographic data can be found at: http://dnb.d-nb.de

All rights reserved. This publication may not be reproduced, stored in a retrieval system or transmitted, in any form or by any means, electronic, mechanical, photocopying, recording or otherwise, without the prior permission of the publishers.

Das Werk einschließlich aller seiner Teile ist urheberrechtlich geschützt. Jede Verwertung außerhalb der Grenzen des Urheberrechtsgesetzes ist ohne Zustimmung des Verlages unzulässig und strafbar. Dies gilt insbesondere für Vervielfältigungen, Übersetzungen, Mikroverfilmungen und die Einspeicherung und Bearbeitung in elektronischen Systemen.

Die Wiedergabe von Gebrauchsnamen, Handelsnamen, Warenbezeichnungen usw. in diesem Werk berechtigt auch ohne besondere Kennzeichnung nicht zu der Annahme, dass solche Namen im Sinne der Warenzeichen- und Markenschutz-Gesetzgebung als frei zu betrachten wären und daher von jedermann benutzt werden dürften.

Die Informationen in diesem Werk wurden mit Sorgfalt erarbeitet. Dennoch können Fehler nicht vollständig ausgeschlossen werden und die Diplomica Verlag GmbH, die Autoren oder Übersetzer übernehmen keine juristische Verantwortung oder irgendeine Haftung für evtl. verbliebene fehlerhafte Angaben und deren Folgen.

Alle Rechte vorbehalten

© Anchor Academic Publishing, Imprint der Diplomica Verlag GmbH
Hermannstal 119k, 22119 Hamburg
http://www.diplomica-verlag.de, Hamburg 2016
Printed in Germany

"Curmudgeons speak up because they have to, because it's become critically important for them to tell the truth as they see it. Telling the truth is as natural to them once more as it was when they were children. The fact that no one cares to listen is inconsequential. Curmudgeons speak up, raise their voices, stand for something too right to be silent about anymore, whatever the cost, despite a world that deals with what it doesn't want to hear by crucifying the messenger. Increasingly these days, they're being called by another name: whistleblower." -- Lionel Fisher

Contents

1. **Introduction** 9
   1.1. Research Question 9
   1.2. Research Design 10
   1.3. Case Selection 11
   1.4. Data Analysis 11
2. **The Case** 12
3. **Whistleblowing** 15
   3.1. What and when about whistleblowing 15
   3.2. Internal and external whistleblowing 18
4. **Theoretical part** 19
   4.1. A model to assess the factors, influencing the whistleblowing intentions by Keil et al. 19
   4.2. 2A model for assessing the effectiveness of whistleblowing by Neil & Miceli (1995) 24
5. **Application to NZA case** 29
   5.1. The NZA case, according to Keil et al. 29
   5.2. Applying the effective whistle-blowing model to the NZA case 31
   5.3. Whistleblowing program costs and benefits 33
6. **Conclusion** 35
7. **Recommendation/Discussion** 37
8. **References** 41
9. **Appendix** 43
   Summary 1 43
   Summary 2 44
   Summary 3 45
   Summary 4 50
   Summary 5 52
   Summary 6 55
   Summary 7 57
   Summary 8 58
   Appendix A. Social processing model of whistle-blowing decisions 60

1. Introduction

This phrase describes the whisteblowing situation quite accurately. Whisteblowers are necessary to introduce change into a company when wrongdoings are identified. They are the first employees within a company, who witness and show wrongdoings that arise in the everyday dealings of a company. However, they are often ignored by their colleagues, supervisors and the company.

Within this research the issues that arise from neglecting the information provided by whistleblowers and ignoring the wrongdoing is illustrated using the case of "de Nederlandse Zorgautoreit", henceforth NZA. It will be shown, which the key variables related to whisteblowing are, from the perspective of a potential whistleblower as well as from a company's perspective. Finally, it is concluded what went wrong in the NZA case and recommendations are provided.

1.1. Research Question

Whisteblowing has a high impact on society as a whole. It is therefore relevant to investigate why a person decides to blow the whistle and what role the company plays in the process. We can learn from the mistakes made in the past to prevent them in the present. Within this research I will therefore analyze a whisteblowing case concerning "de Nederlandse Zorg autoriteit". This paper will analyze the case by using existing academic models. This allows us to draw conclusions about what went wrong within the NZA case. These models show the decision making process of the whistleblower and what role the company plays in it.

From this point forward the organizational willingness to change is introduced. This depends on several variables that will be explained as well. These variables will determine whether a company will actually change its behavior and terminate the wrongdoing.

This paper has therefore the following research question:

What went wrong in the NZA case according to the current dominant academic models and what could NZA have done to prevent it?

In order to provide a coherent answer and analysis sub-questions were defined and elaborated on in the following:

- Which factors influenced the whistleblower's decision to blow the whistle?
- What was the role of the organization in this decision-making process?
- Was there an organizational willingness to change and terminate the wrongdoing?
- What are the cost/benefits of terminating the wrongdoing and what are the current costs of NZA?
- What could have prevented the current outcome?

Once these questions have been answered possible recommendations will be given what NZA could have done to prevent this situation. Although a single case study has a low generalizability it is still academically relevant to determine the pivotal variables in this case study. In addition, companies that take this research into account might be capable to understand the context of this type of situations and prevent the latter.

1.2. Research Design

The intention of this research is to see what went wrong in the NZA case. Furthermore analyzing this recent case, ended with a suicide could lead to deriving important recommendations about how to motivate employees to share information about the wrongdoings they witnessed and how to ensure that this information is not going to be ignored by the organization.

For that purpose the current dominant models will be applied to the case. Thereby I want to assess both the whistleblower's decision-making process and the organizational reaction on it. The problem with models is that they have restrictions. In addition, the analysis of the case could identify additional variables that have been omitted in previous research as well as assess areas for future research.

The latter is known as the omitted variables problem. When using models, certain variables can either be over-or-underestimated due to the missing factor (Gerring, 2004). In the current case study the strength of the variables are not known. Therefore, it is only possible to check whether certain variables are missing.

In addition, the choice to conduct a case study already gives limitations. Since I use existing models it is a crucial case study. This is a case study that investigates a phenomenon against the background of a received theory (Gerring, 2012). The use of a crucial case study leads to both internal and external validity threats. There are a lot of threats. The most important ones will be described below.

The first threat is ambiguous temporal precedence. This is the situations in which there is no certainty about the order of occurrence of the variables. Therefore, no conclusion can be drawn about the possible "cause" and "effect". We have temporal variation. The problem with the current case study is that we do not exactly know what happened when. Therefore, temporal precedence could be a serious threat. Yet, the main purpose of this research is to know whether certain variables could have prevented the situation in this case. Therefore, this research does not look at whether one variable preceeds the other. However, we have to take into account that the precedence of one variable could ultimately lead to the occurrence of another. This situation does lead to a validity threat and is a limitation in the research.

Secondly, this research might suffer from selection bias. The problem with a crucial case study is that the level of generalizability is rather low. Indeed, the research done in the area of whistleblowing shows very generic models, while the cases itself are very specific. It could be that the specific situations in the NZA case study could lead to certain variables playing a more important role and others playing a less important role. The first problem is that the models do not measure the strength of the variables. The second problem is that NZA might be very case-specific leading to a very low generalizability.

History is another internal validity problem. We do have temporal and maybe even some spatial variation. Therefore, certain "acts of nature" might have influenced the case study that eventually led to the current outcome. Since this research is based on models, the variables might therefore be biased. In addition, this research might not take into account variables that have (pivotal) influence.

Maturation should also be taken into account. This case study involves persons who mature during the period of case study. Since we have temporal and spatial variation the subjects might change during the course of the current case study.

Other validity problems such as testing effects, statistical regression, attrition and non compliance do not play an important role within this current case study.

1.3. Case Selection

As already mentioned, the main focus will be on the NZA case. Next to that several other cases will be used to illustrate a certain parameter or to provide a motivation to a certain recommendation. The reason why this research uses the NZA case is because it is fairly new and not much (possibly even not at all) research has yet been done. It is therefore a very interesting case study that might provide answers to many unanswered or yet to be answered questions and provide critical recommendations in regard to dealing with wrongdoings. The data about the NZA case is acquired by using newspapers, news reports and blogs. Especially the Dutch paper "NRC Handelsblad" provides extensive information since it has access to all of the information Arthur Gotlieb also gave to NZA.

However since this information is due to now not yet made publicly available, we cannot exclude the possibility that some information is still left unconsidered, possibly leading to not entirely objective conclusions and biased model analysis. I tried to gather as much information as possible in order to minimize this possibility.

1.4. Data Analysis

Once the case information has been summarized, I will use three models to assess the decision making process whether or not to blow the whistle and the processing of the information provided by the whistleblower, followed by change in the organization and terminating the wrongdoing within the NSA case. From that point forward I will draw conclusions and give possible recommendations about both the case study and the models.

2. The Case

A typical example of a whistleblowing that is not followed by changes in the organization but only associated with "terrible experience" of the whistleblower is NZA case discussed in the following. In order to assess the consequences of ignoring the reported wrongdoings and make a statement about what went wrong in the this case, a brief description of the case is provided below.

This case shows a peculiar situation within a company claiming to be a learning organization. A learning organization is a company or institution that promotes the development of new knowledge or insights that have the potential to influence possible future behavior and can change existing norms and values within a company (Senge and Suzuki, 1994).

The peculiarity lies in the fact that there was a whistleblower that promoted change within the company but nothing really happened. How is it possible that an organization such as NZA which claims to be a learning organization did not listen to the complaints from its own employee? To answer this question we need detailed information about the case itself that is then going to be mapped against the currently dominant whisteblowing decision-making and whistleblowing processing models.

However, it is better to take many small steps in the right direction than to make a great leap forward to only stumble backward. I, therefore, start by explaining the case.

This case involves a senior manager within the organization of NZA named Arthur Gotlieb. The NZA is an organization that has a monopoly position as legislator in the healthcare market. The main activities of this institution involve the determination of the amount of healthcare to be provided by health care institutions, the price and the quality (Dohmen and Wester, 2014).

For a period of thirteen years long Gotlieb was one of the people responsible for the recognition of treatments involving expensive medicines. In this period, Gotlieb recognized a lot of flaws within the system of NZA. The result was a file of 600 pages, supported by 3 gigabyte of proof such as internal correspondence, documents, pictures and audio files. There were five main issues.

The first problem was the so called "clean desk" rule in which employees were only allowed to leave their jobs and go home after people literally cleaned their desks. The pictures Gotlieb made showed something else. Desk offices, paper bins and printers contained a lot of private information. Access to this information was therefore easy and because there were (and are) a lot of temporary employees active in the company itself the right information could easily end up in the wrong hands.

A second major flaw was that employees that left the NZA started working for companies that they first had to supervise. Since NZA is capable of fining companies that do not obey the rules of the former, an enlaced situation was created. This led to new management members that knew whether they were being supervised and whether NZA was planning on fining them.

A third problem was that it was possible to check the agenda of every person within the company. This included possible resumes and other private information of persons. The letter and resume of director Paul Frencken who applied in June 2009 could be read by everyone. Temporary employees had access as well.

Fourthly, every employee had access to the so called "V-drive". This drive was created for employees to share information. This information on the V-drive was supposed to be there only temporary. However, employees did not delete the information which led to 300 gigabytes of information that remained stored on the drive. This included patient files, audio files of hearings and more private information. Even people who only worked at NZA during the holidays could access this information.

The last complaint of Arthur Gotlieb was about another part of the network, the so called W-drive. This drive contained information such as high quality pictures of director signatures, which could easily be counterfeited. Gotlieb complained that this part of the network was not protected. Temporary employees and people having a holiday job could access this information.

Arthur Gotlieb warned his senior managers quite frequently about all these major flaws. The management did not do anything with the information Gotlieb gave them. Indeed, they even ignored him for a period amounting to four years. During that period, Gotlieb got bullied by the same managers who did not listen and even tried to get rid of him. A good example is that they gave him a heavy work load which could be compared with a 2.0 Full-time equivalent (better known as FTE). Gotlieb complained four times about this job pressure. The management responded by giving him even more work. In addition, Gotlieb got a lot of negative feedback on his job performance and people never responded to his emails.

At the 10th of January 2014 Gotlieb delivered the file of 600 pages to the NZA. On the 22nd of January he committed suicide. He died at the age of fifty. Gotlieb is described as a person who loved his work. Before the whole situation started the feedback on his job performance was positive. In addition, people describe him as having a good sense of humor.

The Dutch government has started an investigation led by minister Schippers who is responsible for healthcare. Conclusions have yet to be drawn, but the first result of the external whisteblowing has emerged. The board of directors has withdrawn themselves from their position.

In the next section three dominant models according to the literature, regarding the whistle-blowing process are described. The first model from Keil et al. (2010) focuses on the decision-making process, which precedes the actual whistle-blowing act of a person. In case the potential whistleblower decides to blow the whistle by communicating the wrongdoing internally, the second model should be applied to assess the processing of the information and whether it led to a change in the organization and termination of the wrongdoing. It thereby indentifies the factors that make whistle-blowing 'effective' (Near and Miceli, 1995). After introducing the models, the academic relevance and empirical evidence regarding the value of the models will be discussed. Based on this relevance, both empirical and academic, a consideration will be made about if and how these models are useful to apply to the NZA case.

3. Whistleblowing

In this section some of the elementary aspects of whistleblowing will be elaborated. The following will be discussed:

- Whistleblower definition
- When is someone a whistleblower
- Internal and external whistleblowing

3.1. What and when about whistleblowing

Whistleblowing has the following definition in the US Whistleblower Protection Act 1989: a present or former employee discloses information which former employee discloses information "which the employee reasonably believes evidences a violation of any law, rule, or regulation, or gross mismanagement, a gross waste of funds, an abuse of authority, or a substantial and specific danger to public health or safety.' (Lennane, 2012, p.1)

The term whistleblowing is becoming commonplace. It is a term that is gladly used by journalists, is often prominent in headlines and is used by them in a variety of contexts in which alleged misconduct is exposed. It is important to keep the term whistleblowing close to what it essentially is, namely informing, and keep it free from prejudice (corrupt individual turned informer, sneaks, spies, etc). There is a risk that whistleblowing will become interchangeable with, and not recognized as a special case of, informing. There are three major goals a whistleblower can have, these are:

- Informing; the release of information is done deliberately and with the aim of achieving a disclosure.
- Accusation; identifies perceived wrongdoing, typically a bad news message about misconduct, incompetence, fraud, etc. alleged to have been ignored and/or covered up. In any case an accusation is being made towards some person or organization.
- Dissent (disagreement); when faced with wrongdoing, a person can choose to disagree with the observed misconduct. During this there are three options which are mentioned in the paragraph below.

Hirschman (1970) has identified three major response categories a whistleblower can have when it comes to organizational misconduct. These are labeled exit, loyalty and voice. Exit is to distance yourself from a problem, voice is to express your concern or disagreement. He presented exit as the standard response to dissatisfaction with economic entities, or leaving your position by seeking a transfer or by resignation. Voice, he claimed, is the usual way to deal with dysfunctional social and political organizations. In both cases the means of expression are mechanisms to relieve the individual's discontent and to give signals that will allow the organization to improve the situation.

Below is a schematic overview of the different actions to take when a person stays (voice) or go's (exit).

Table 1: Dissent aspect and the exit dimension (Jubb, 1999)

Expression of the concern (voice)	Nature of the perceived activity triggering the concern			
	Illegal, immoral or illegitimate		Not illegal immoral or illegitimate	
	Exit dimension			
	Stay	Go	Stay	Go
External dissent to someone who can take action	External whistle-blowing	Exit with public protest[b]	Secret sharing	Exit with secret sharing
Internal dissent to someone who can take action	Internal whistle-blowing	Protest during exit interview[h]	Employee participation, grievance	Explain reason for resignation in exit
Dissent in some other form	Discussion, confrontation with wrongdoer	Exit with notice to wrongdoer	Sabotage, strikes	Sabotage, strikes with exit
No expressed dissent	Inactive observation[e]	Inactive departure	Silent disgruntlement	Silent departure

Lennane (2012) identifies a whistleblower as a principled organizational dissenter. The whistleblower acts on principle when something is observed that conflicts between immediate authority (employer) and higher authority (norms, values, justice, in public interest). The reaction that follows is organizational, as it arises from the organization being challenged on its authoritive power. Finally the whistleblower dissents from the culture, internal principles and believes of an organization.

Jubb (1999) gives an overview of previous research into the topic of whistleblowing. Below are a number of definitions formulated by previous researchers:

> "Whistleblowing is the act, by an employee or officer of any institution, profit or non-profit, private or public, of informing the public about a belief that either (s)he has been ordered to perform, or (s)he has obtained knowledge that the institution is engaged in, activities which (a) cause unnecessary harm to third parties, (b) are in violation of human rights, or (c) run counter to the defined purpose of the institution" (Bowie and Duska, 1990).

> whistleblowing by internal auditors is "The unauthorized disclosure in the public interest by internal auditors of audit results, findings, opinions, or information acquired in the course of performing their duties and relating to questionable practices" (Chambers, 1995, pp. 192-193).

"The whistleblower is a concerned citizen, totally, or predominantly motivated by notions of public interest, who initiates of her or his own free will, an open disclosure about significant wrongdoing directly perceived in a particular occupational role, to a person or agency capable of investigating the complaint and facilitating the correction of wrongdoing" (De Maria, 1994, p. 3).

"Whistleblowing, defined as disclosing questionable practice involving the organization or its members, may be either internal or external. Internal whistleblowing involves informing relevant organization members about wrongdoing. External whistleblowing involves going outside the organization . . . to voice concerns over an organizational wrongdoing" (Chiasson et al., 1995, p. 24).

". . . we defined whistle-blowing to mean 'the disclosure by organisation members (former or current) of illegal, immoral or illegitimate practices under the control of their employers, to persons or organisations that may be able to effect action' " (Miceli and Near, 1992, p. 15).

Collecting a number of definitions and presenting them in a schematic fashion gives the following table:

Table 2: Overview of whistleblowing aspects

	Bowie & Duska (1990)	Chambers (1995)	De Maria (1994)	Miceli & Near (1992)	Chiasson et al. (1995)
Action					
- Reporting	X	X	X	X	X
- Intended					
- Unauthorized		X			X
- Voluntary			X		X
By					
- Employee	X				
- Org. member		X	X	X	X
Motive					
- Moral motive	X				
- In public interest		X	X		
What					
- Illegality				X	
- Immoral acts		X		X	X
- Qualifiers					
• occurs in org.	X				
• in org. control					
• involves org. member				X	
To					
- Internal authorities					X
- External authorities					
- General public	X		X		X
- Entity able to effect a remedy			X	X	

3.2. Internal and external whistleblowing

A distinction can be made between two types of whistleblower, namely internal and external. An internal whistleblower informs misconduct to persons within the target organization. This can be done in accordance with routine procedures to a designated superior or within prescribed arrangements for non-routine situations, such as notifying an ethics officer. The disclosure can also go outside of set procedures (unauthorized) and be made to someone higher up the chain of command or an influential colleague, being someone outside the normal chain of command, for instance an approach to a director or to senior personnel in some other division or section.

An external whistleblower reports observed misconduct to an outside agency, such as the media, protective agencies, lawyers or politicians. It is often the case that whistle-blowers only go externally after their complaint has been ignored internally. Such was the case in a survey studied by Lennane (2012) in which 91% of subjects did not receive a proper response from inside the organization and resorted to an outside agency. A survey done by Soeken and Soeken (1987) showed a similar outcome (for 80.5% the initial internal complaint was considered unsuccessful). The below table gives an overview of to whom the observed misconduct was first reported.

Table 3: First contacted in the case of observed misconduct. (Soeken and Soeken, 1987)

To Whom	Number	Percent
Immediate supervisor	30	36.6
Head of firm/agency	14	17.1
Newspaper/Radio/Press	11	13.4
Hot Line	6	7.3
Congressional Representative	4	4.9
Government Accountability Project	1	1.2
Other	16	19.5

4. Theoretical part

4.1. A model to assess the factors, influencing the whistleblowing intentions by Keil et al.

It is important for a company to motivate its employees to use internal ways instead of making wrongdoings public, as stated in section 3.2. Therefore it should be aware and make use of the intervening mechanisms through which whistleblowing intentions are formed. These factors can be explained using the middle-range theory of whistleblowing by Keil et al. This model has been developed, tested and accordingly adjusted and as such is the dominant model explaining whistleblowing intentions.

The central explanatory variable of this model is the perceived "benefit-to-cost differential", henceforth BCD. (Keil et al., 2010) It is defined as the net difference between the perceived costs and expected benefits of whistleblowing from the perspective of a potential whistleblower. It is claimed that a witness of a wrongdoing would weigh the cost and benefits, associated with the whistleblowing and make a decision based on their difference. Therefore this decision making process will result in whistleblowing only in case the expected benefits outweigh the costs associated with whistleblowing. The key question is then which factors influence the BCD. For the selection of factors the social information processing framework of whistleblowing developed by Gundlach et al. is used. (Keil et al., 2010) This framework will be explained in the following.

Using the social information processing framework of Gundlach et al (2003) to identify factors influencing the decision-making process whether or not to blow the whistle

By integrating power, justice and pro-social theories, Gundlach et al., (2003) tried to set up a social information processing framework. This framework tends to capture all the factors that are influencing the decision-making process of an individual whether or not to blow the whistle when identifying organizational wrongdoing. Gundlach et al., (2003) divide their model in interpersonal and intrapersonal factors. Interpersonal factors form the main part of the model and will be explained first. Intrapersonal factors could influence the interpersonal factors as will be explained later. The model itself is not shown in this section because the focus lies on the model of Keil et al., (2010) but for a better understanding of this part the model can be viewed in the summary in appendix A.

When an individual recognizes organizational wrongdoing, their emotions and their decisions whether they should blow the whistle are influenced by the cost and benefit analysis they make regarding the act of whistle-blowing. Besides of weighing the psychological and economic costs and benefits, potential whistleblowers also add attributions and responsibility judgments to their decision-making process. If a potential whistleblower attributes the wrongdoing to internal, stable and controllable causes, they will probably hold the wrongdoer(s) responsible and therefore they are more likely to decide to blow the whistle (Gundlach et al., 2003).

Social influence of the wrongdoer could also influence the decision-making process of a potential whistleblower. This social influence can be specified as the use of impression management tactics to manipulate the decision-making. These impression management tactics form the intrapersonal factors in the model. Both, defensive impression management and offensive impression management appear in the model. Defensive impression management means that the excuses and justifications made by the wrongdoer influence the (interpersonal) attributions by defining them as 'uncontrollable' and 'unstable'. As earlier stated, perceived controllable and stable causes should lead to whistleblowing and therefore this defensive impression tactic lowers this incentive. The second tactic is the offensive impression management. When a wrongdoer uses retaliation and threats, the potential-whistleblower will increase judgments of the responsibility of the wrongdoer and therefore encourages the actual whistleblowing. However, if this tactic leads to a high amount of fear against the wrongdoer the potential whistleblower could decide to not do it.

Besides of the intrapersonal and interpersonal factors there are two interfering factors added in the model: the power of both the wrongdoer and the potential whistle-blower and the credibility of the presentation of the impression management tactics. For example if the perceived power of the wrongdoer is high, blowing the whistle causes fear and therefore the potential whistleblower could decide not to blow the whistle. Also, when the presentation of an impression management tactic is perceived as non-credible it is more likely that the whistle is blown.

The seven factors influencing the BCD according to Keil et al.

From the framework of Gundlach et al (2003), seven factors are claimed to be the key factors influencing the BCD and therefore the whistleblowing intentions. The focus on these seven factors is chosen based on the dominant theory and literature and is necessary in order to practicality. (Keil et al., 2010)

The seven factors that companies need to consider when employing a whistleblowing program are shortly explained in the following.

Personal reporting responsibility is referred to as the degree of formally prescribed responsibility to report a whistleblower is associated with. It is claimed that a prescribed reporting responsibility enhances the likelihood of observing and reporting a wrongdoing. (Miceli and Near, 1984) Several studies develop models, according to which personal reporting responsibility has a direct influence on the whistleblowing intentions. (Smith et al., 2001; Keil et al., 2004). However here it is claimed that the BCD plays a mediating role in the relationship between personal reporting responsibility and the whistleblowing intentions.

The second factor that is believed to influence the whistleblowing intentions is trust in the supervisor. The extent to which the integrity of the immediate supervisor is trusted is observed to influence the upward communication likelihood of wrongdoings. Higher trust in the supervisor is associated with higher tendency to inform the latter in case a wrongdoing is observed. (Gaines, 1980) Higher support from and trust in supervisors is related to more whistleblowing. (Blackburn, 1988; Graham, 1986). Here higher trust is related to lower perceived costs of reporting the wrongdoing due to less perceived risk for reprisal from the supervisor. This increases the BCD and has therefore positive impact on the likelihood of whistleblowing.

The ability to hide the information about a wrongdoing is defined as the likelihood of no one else knowing unless the potential whistleblower reveals the information. This factor is based on the agency theory and it is found and empirically proved that information asymmetry lowers the whistleblowing intentions. (Harrell and Harrison, 1994; Tuttle et al., 1997). Again here BCD is claimed to mediate the relationship between the ability to hide information and the whistleblowing intentions.

It is believed that if whistleblowing does not require revealing one's personality, the costs associated with whistleblowing from the potential whistleblower perspective decrease. The forth factor believed to influence the whistleblowing intentions indirectly is therefore reporting anonymity. It is suggested that anonymity is preferred even in the presence of formal reporting channels. (Miceli and Near, 1992).

An expected benefit and also the main benefit (Miceli and Near, 1994) of whistleblowing from a potential whistleblower perspective is the willingness to correct the reported wrongdoing. Therefore management responsiveness referred to as the management responsiveness towards solving the wrongdoing plays a key role in determining the BCD and thereby influences the whistleblowing intentions. If the whistleblower perceived management responsiveness to be high, it is associated with higher likelihood that the appropriate measures will be employed and that the whistleblower will be protected from retaliation. This increases the likelihood of him/her reporting the wrongdoing accordingly. (Dozier and Miceli, 1985; Graham, 1986).

The organizational climate should also encourage internal whistleblowing. The sixth factor of the framework is the organizational climate conduciveness, defined as the degree to which organizational policies and climate encourages wrongdoings' reporting. More conducivenesses in terms of existence of forms, policies and deployed procedures for internal reporting of wrongdoing would increase the perception of whistleblowing support and decrease the costs associated with whistleblowing accordingly. (Micheli & Near, 1992) On the other hand the absence of the latter would lead to organizational silence. (Morrison and Milliken, 2000)

Next to management responsiveness, senior management attachment influences the whistleblowing intentions through the BCD. If the management is directly involved in the wrongdoing the costs associated with whistleblowing increase due to fear of reprisal. (Conlee and Tesser, 1973; Johnson et al., 1974; Tesser and Rossen, 1975) Furthermore it can decrease the expected benefits as it will be associated with higher likelihood of ignorance of the information as well as low willingness to charge. (Keil et al., 2010) In sum this would decrease the BCD and thereby lower the whistleblowing intentions.

The model overview is provided in figure 1.

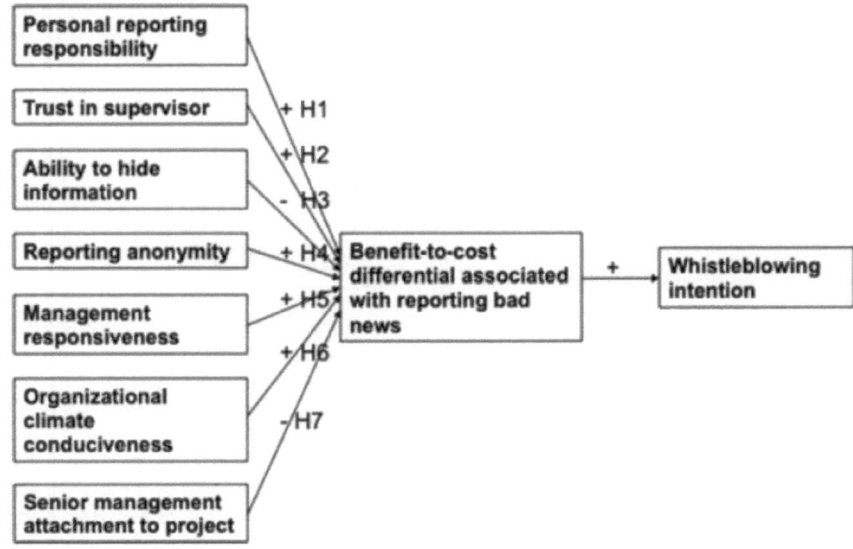

Figure 1: Research model for the whistleblowing intentions. (Keil et al., 2010)

All seven factors as introduced above influence the whistleblowing intentions indirectly, as the BCD is claimed to mediate the respective relationships. Two of the factors are perceived as increasing the perceived costs and decreasing the expected benefits of whistleblowing, associated with decrease in the BCD thus having a negative impact on the whistleblowing intentions. Those are the ability to hide information and the senior management attachment. All other factors are claimed to positively influence the BCD thereby increasing the whistleblowing intentions.

Testing the validity of the model

In order to validate the model an empirical test with 132 IT project managers from the Project Management Institute's Atlanta Chapter, henceforth PMI using a conjoint research design was performed, in which participants are presented hypothetical scenarios with varying levels of the seven factors. This enables them to provide an answer not to simplified solutions but weigh various factors associated with the decisions. The participants were asked to assess the BCD for each scenario as well as the likelihood for reporting the wrongdoing.

The independent variables were the seven factors as introduced in the previous, including personal reporting responsibility, trust in supervisor, ability to hide information, level of anonymity, management responsiveness, organizational climate conduciveness and senior management attachment level as perceived from the respondents based on the provided scenario. Each of these variables was then varied within the scenarios between a high and a low level, using semantic differential scales. The ultimate dependent variable was the likelihood of reporting the wrongdoing. As BCD is claimed to mediate this effect, a measure is included to asses it in the developed scenarios. The power and relevance of BCD as a mediator is assessed via Sobel mediation tests. (Keil et al., 2010)

As the approximate response rate is 26.4% a test for non-response bias is conducted. However there are no significant differences observed. Therefore the assumption can be made that the non-response bias are no threat to the findings.

Eight scenarios are developed in total, as it is the smallest number of conjoint profiles needed to provide accurate and reliable analysis according to the fractional factorial design conducted. So, every respondent was asked to evaluate eight scenarios.

The eight hypothesizes are tested using hierarchical regression. The control variables, such as years of work experience, gender etc. explain 9% of the variance in whistleblowing intention. Adding up the seven whistleblowing factors increases the explanatory power to 25%. Finally, considering the BCD as well leads to explanation of 52% of the variance. This illustrates the importance of the BCD when investigating whistleblowing intentions. Thus companies are required to employ measures aiming at high BCD by minimizing the perceived costs and maximizing the expected benefits associated with whistleblowing. (Keil et al., 2010)

Results and revised model

Analysis of the results determines the need for adjustment of the model. Two of the seven factors – personal reporting responsibility and reporting anonymity, support the hypothesis of full mediation by the BCD, thus having no direct effect on the whistleblowing intentions. Furthermore BCD partially mediates the effect on whistleblowing intentions on three other factors – trust in supervisor, management responsiveness and organizational climate conduciveness. The last two factors – ability to hide information and senior management attachment are not mediated by the BCD. The ability to hide information turns out to have neither direct nor indirect effect on the whistleblowing intentions and has been therefore withdrawn from the revised model. Senior management attachment has a direct influence on the whistleblowing intentions but other than expected it promotes whistleblowing. (Keil et al., 2010) This could be explained by the perception of potential whistleblowers that the management is highly involved, wants to know about wrongdoings and is willing to correct those. The three most potent factors according to the conducted test are trust in supervisor, management responsiveness and organizational climate conduciveness.

The revised model is shown in Figure 2.

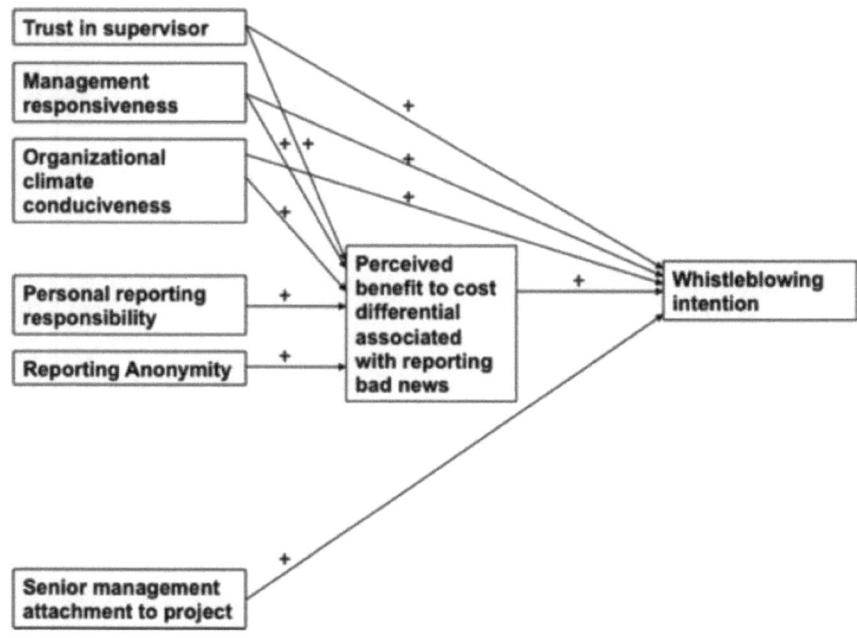

Figure 2: Revised model to explain whistleblowing intentions. (Keil et al., 2010)

Limitations

However further investigation is needed to validate the revised model. It is questionable to which extent the hypothetical scenarios generalize the actual organizational setting. Furthermore the representative power of the PMI's Atlanta Chapter is an issue. The appropriation of the selection of and focus on the seven aforementioned factors should be further investigated. Keil et al. suggests for example possible inclusion of additional factors, such as strategic importance. (Keil et al., 2010)

4.2. 2A model for assessing the effectiveness of whistleblowing by Neil & Miceli (1995)

While the previous section focused on the decision-making part of the whistle-blowing process, this section is about the 'effectiveness' of the whistle-blowing act that is the consequent processing of the acquired information about the wrongdoing and the corresponding actions. Ineffective whistle-blowing benefits neither the whistle-blower as the organization and therefore it is important to know which variables influence the outcome of the act. The central model used in this section is the model containing the variables that influence the outcome of whistle-blowing from Near & Miceli (1995)

Whistle-blowing could lead to positive changes if handled in the right way. Effective whistle-blowing is defined as "the extent to which the questionable or wrongful practice (or omission) is terminated at least partly because of whistle-blowing and within a reasonable time frame" (Near and Miceli, 1995). According to Near & Miceli (1995) the termination of the wrongdoing depends on the willingness to change within the organization. If the wrongdoing act has been terminated this could lead to either higher organizational performance in the future, as to a better control of the elements in the external environment. The model exists out of two different types of variables that are influencing the impact of whistle-blowing: individual variables and situational variables.

Individual variables

There are two major factors which influence the content of the individual variables: Power and credibility. The model, which is shown in figure 3, contains three types of individual factors: 1) characteristics of the whistle-blower, 2) characteristics of the complaint recipient and 3) characteristics of the wrongdoer.

The characteristics of the whistle-blower are expected to positively influence the whistle-blowing effectiveness when managers, co-workers, and the complaint recipient perceive the whistle-blower as credible and powerful. Also whistle-blowers who are not afraid to identify themselves are more likely to be effective. Second, if complaint recipients are supporting the whistle-blowing, effectiveness will increase as the complaint recipient has a higher level of credibility and power. At last, effectiveness will increase if the wrongdoer has less power and/or credibility.

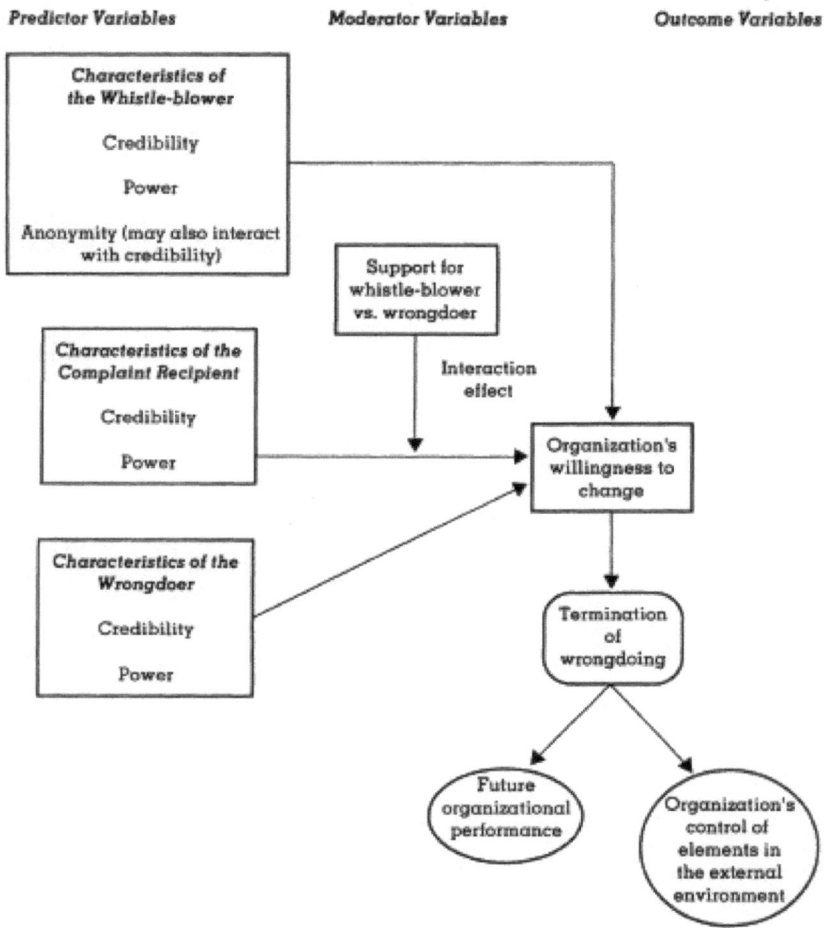

Figure 3: Individual variables that affect the outcome of whistleblowing. (Near & Miceli, 1995)

Situational variables

Two more variables are influencing the organizations' willingness to change and with that the termination of wrongdoing. First there are characteristics of the wrongdoing followed by the characteristics of the wrongdoing. The second part of the model, containing these situational variables is shown in figure 4.

When first looking at the characteristics of the wrongdoing three propositions are made. First effectiveness of internal whistle-blowing is likely to decrease if the wrongdoing is highly dependent on the wrongdoing act, but it will increase if the whistle is blown externally. Second, effectiveness will increase if the report is convincing and also if the wrongdoing act is illegal and unambiguous.

Four organizational factors are expected to be influential. First effectiveness increases if the act is perceived as appropriate by the organization or informal norms. Second effectiveness increases if the organizational climate encourages whistle-blowing. Third effectiveness increases when an organization has a bureaucratic structure and if the organization uses formal mechanisms to encourage internal whistle-blowing. The last variable concerns the power of the organization in the external environment. If this power is low, whistle-blowing has more potential to be effective.

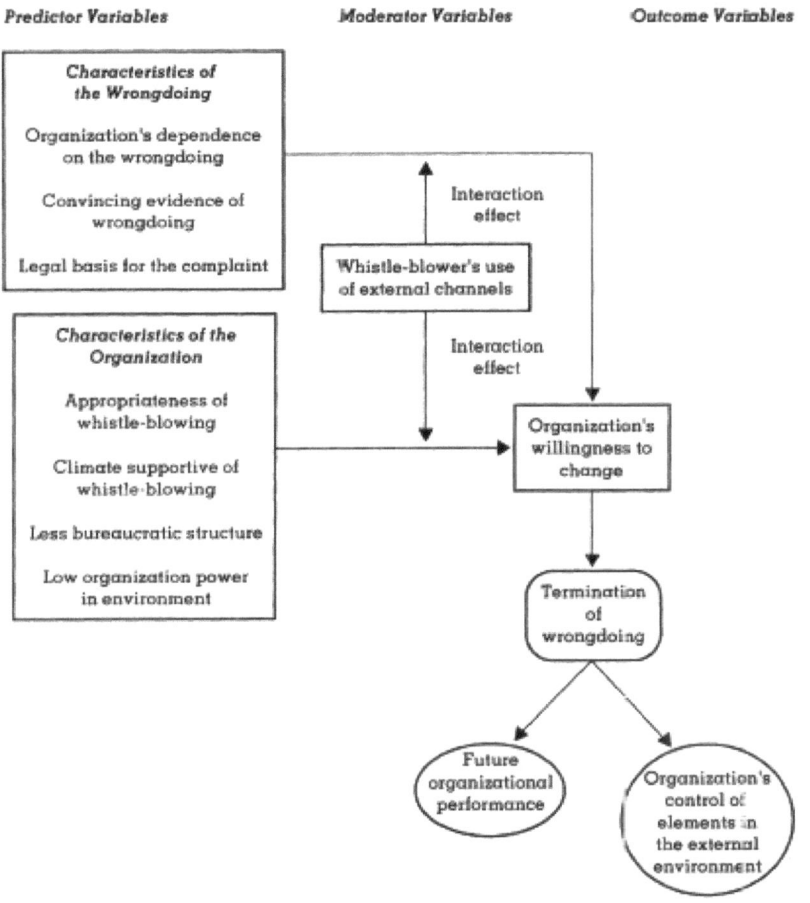

Figure 4: Situational variables that affect the outcome of whistleblowing. (Near & Miceli, 1995)

Testing the validity of the model

Unfortunately the model as a whole has not been empirically tested yet, though parts of the model are tested by (Miceli and Near, 2002) by conducting three field studies. In these studies whistle-blowers were asked to give their perceptions about the effectiveness of their whistle-blowing. Three independent variables, provided from the model, were tested and were respectively 1) position power, 2) organizational dependence of the wrongdoing, and 3) the complaints recipient power. These variables were expected to predict the termination of wrongdoing.

Two hypotheses were set regarding the first variable, position power. The first hypothesis was: "Whistle-blowing will be more effective when it is role-prescribed." And the second hypothesis was "Whistle-blowing will be more effective when whistleblowers experience lower levels of retaliation.". Both hypotheses were supported by all of the three studies and therefore it could be said that the power position, when looking at retaliation level and job prescription, leads to (better) termination of the wrongdoing.

The third hypothesis regarding organizational dependence of the wrongdoing was only measured by looking at internal whistle-blowing and was worded as "When whistleblowers do not use channels external to the organization, they are more effective when the wrongdoing is of lesser magnitude." The results showed that whistle-blowers who perceived the wrongdoing as from less magnitude were experiencing a higher level of termination of the wrongdoing.

The last hypotheses regarding the power of the complaint recipient was stated as "Whistle-blowing will be more effective when whistleblowers who use internal channels report wrongdoing to complaint recipients of high status or legitimacy." The results showed that a report of a wrongdoing act to a complaint recipient of higher status or legitimacy was more likely to be effective.

Conclusion

Concluding from this section it can be said that empirical evidence of the value of the model is partly present. The variables that are researched (position power, organizational dependence of the wrongdoing and power of the complaint recipient) are all supported. Unfortunately additional research is needed to make a proper valuation of the model. For example the last hypothesis about power of the complaint recipient was supported, but there is no information available about the impact of effectiveness if complaint recipient and wrongdoer are the same party. However seen this is the only existing model about effectiveness of whistle-blowing and there is also no evidence which devaluates the model it could be used to apply to the NZA case.

After the two models explain the whistleblowing decision making process and the consequent actions formally, the situation at NZA according to them, will be taken into consideration.

5. Application to NZA case

5.1. The NZA case, according to Keil et al.

From the NZA case it can be concluded that the whistleblowing intentions led to whistleblowing in this particular case. Therefore the assumption is made that the BCD is positive, hence the perceived benefits outweigh the expected costs from the whistleblower's perspective. Since no monetary benefits for whistleblowing were employed within the company, the benefits that Arthur Gotlieb associated with whistleblowing could have only been the expected change and the consequent improvement of the current situation. The costs could have been fear of reprisal, fear of losing his job or hierarchical position as senior manager, harassment from colleagues etc. However a little evidence is provided on the expected costs associated with the whistleblowing from Arthus Gotlieb's perspective. Therefore only assumptions can be made. We assume that Arthur Gotlieb was aware of all of the fore mentioned risks.

Since he blew the whistle, conducting a report of 600 pages, the net difference of benefits and costs associated with whistleblowing from his perspective must have been positive. We assume that this is due to the high perceived benefit of improvement of the current situation, that is improvement in data security of the sensible data.

This is again confirmed by his suicide after acknowledging that the organization won't employ any measures for changing the current way of doing things. Furthermore the organization refuses to recognize the issues by ignoring them. The suicide itself can be therefore led back to the fact that the expected benefit that outweighed the costs and led to the whistleblowing, did not turn out to be realized. Therefore the costs overwhelmed Arthur Gotlieb leading to no other solution from his perspective.

However it cannot be claimed that this is the only reason led to the suicide. Other factors and events could have also led to this, such as family issues. Another reason could be also the fact that the realized costs far more overweighed the expected costs for whistleblowing. The unusual extra work load, negative feedback to his work by the top management and the ignorance by colleagues have possibly put Arthur Gotlieb under pressure too much for him to handle. Possible explanation of his suicide can also be his attempt to draw attention and enforce dealing with the issues.

In the following the six factors of the revised model as introduced in the previous section will be mapped against the case to assess their eligibility and completeness for explaining the flow of events.

Personal reporting responsibility is applicable to Arthur Gottlieb's case, since he was a senior manager, responsible for the recognition of treatments involving expensive medicines. Therefore it can be assumed that a part of his job description was reporting. Next to the formally prescribed reporting responsibility, due to his high position in the hierarchy, he should have had also informal reporting responsibility. Since he is likely to be in the position of witnessing wrongdoing, he is implicitly responsible for taking it to the top management. Again this is reassured by the 600 pages report, he issued. It is less likely such a report to be compounded by a person that never had to write a report before. As explained before, this is expected to have increased the whistleblowing intentions by increasing the BCD.

Trust in the supervisor is a difficult factor to assess using the public information available. However Arthur Gotlieb did choose to communicate the issues with the security of sensible data onto the internal ways first, so this speaks for certain amount of trust in the supervisors. The lack of response from the top management and his direct supervisors have certainly led to disappearance of the latter. According to Keil et al. framework trust in the supervisor is one of the key factors having direct and indirect (via the BCD) influence on whistleblowing intentions. However in this particular case such influence cannot be fully observed.

The ability to hide information was withdrawn from the model, after conducting the tests. In this case the ability to hide information did not play significantly important role as well. Arthur Gotlieb frequently reports issues with the data security to his supervisors, so no intention to hide information about a wrongdoing can be seen.

Furthermore anonymity does not seem to be the issue here as well. It is not acquainted that Arthur Gotlieb was trying or aiming at preserving his personality anonym. Mechanisms and procedures for anonym internal whistleblowing are also not apparent.

Management responsiveness or more precise the lack of management responsiveness played a major role at the outlet. In this case the management not only does not respond adequately to the reported issues but moreover ignored and discouraged reporting initiatives. However, when analyzing whistleblowing intentions the focus lies not on the management responsiveness itself but on the management responsiveness as perceived by the potential whistleblower. Since Arthur Gotlieb chose to disclose the wrongdoing to his supervisors first instead of going public, the extent of management responsiveness from his perspective must have been high or high enough. Furthermore he waited for four years before making a public disclosure, which indicates a continuous trust that the management will respond to his reports eventually.

This high expected management responsiveness increases the BCD by increasing the expected benefits and in the same time decreasing the costs associated with whistleblowing as explained in the previous section. The increased BCD increases the whistleblowing intention and can be seen as one of the major factors that have led to the whistleblowing in this case.

Not much can be said about the organizational climate and the organizational climate conduciveness. As stated in the case the organization claims to be a learning organization. However this recent case discloses unwillingness to change. Furthermore it indicates the unwillingness to receive bad news and to search for solutions. Not to underestimate is the climate of punishment when reporting a wrongdoing. Not only that the management did not thank Arthur Gotlieb for his engagement but it overloaded him with additional work and frustrated him with bad feedback on his work. No evidence on employed organizational policies or the existence of forms and procedures for internal reporting of wrongdoing is indicated. On the contrary, this case shows that even when employees search for a way to do that despite of the missing mechanisms, this is being punished. It can be concluded that there is no or very limited organizational climate conduciveness. This would normally decrease the BCD and has a direct negative influence on the whistleblowing intentions. However whether that is the case here, cannot be yet assessed.

The senior management attachment to these issues is very high, as it is in their power to ensure adequate dealing with the sensible information. However since this is crucial for the NZA the senior management is expected to be highly involved, wanting to know about wrongdoings and willing to correct those. However this is not the case for Arthur Gotlieb and his report. Not only the management is not willing to initiate changes but also ignores reported wrongdoings and humbles reporting initiatives. It is again not possible to assess the perception of Arthur Gotlieb. Similarly to management responsiveness, the waiting time of four years indicates somewhat expectations about senior management attachment, which directly enhanced his whistleblowing intentions.

The three most potent factors according to the revised model are trust in supervisor, management responsiveness and organizational climate conduciveness. Taking the available information into consideration the management responsiveness played the most important role in this case. Furthermore for this analysis personal reporting responsibility played a major role in the whistleblowing intentions as well. Reporting anonymity can be withdrawn from the model application in this particular case. The ability to hide information was taken out from the model after conducting the tests. The same applies to the considered NZA case.

5.2. Applying the effective whistle-blowing model to the NZA case

In this section the model of effective whistle-blowing of (Near and Miceli, 1995) will be applied to the NZA case. The goal of using the model is to get a clear sight on the factors that were causing ineffectiveness of the whistle-blowing act of Arthur Gotlieb. It should be mentioned that the outcomes in this whistle-blowing case regarding the wrongdoing is yet hard to measure because the case is still running. However according to the book of Brown, (2008) whistleblowing outcomes are not only about the termination of wrongdoing, but could be looked at from different perspectives, which are interrelated. From the perspective of the whistle-blower it can be said with certainty that the outcome was bad, seen the bullying and suicide. By analyzing the different variables we will try to understand why Arthur Gotlieb was not heard in the first place and why the case is still running and therefore can be seen as ineffective. First the individual factors are explored, followed by the situational factors.

Individual factors

1) Characteristics of the whistle-blower

According to the case, Gotlieb got a lot of negative feedback on his job performance after making his report publicly available, he was also bullied and not taken seriously by his co-workers. The power level of the whistle-blower in this case was not high enough to increase the willingness of the management to change. The power of the management on the other hand was quite strong. First of all they ignored all the facts Gotlieb presented them for a period of four years. On top of that they even bullied Gotlieb and increased his workload. Regarding the credibility of Gotlieb, two things can be mentioned. First the management seems not to deny the credibility of Gotlieb, probably because the evidence is strong, but on the other hand the fact that people were not responding to his e-mails and he was bullied tends to perceived non-credibility.

2) Characteristics of the complaint recipient

The power of the complaint recipient, which was the management of NZA, can be seen as high, because the management is the organizations' main decision-making body towards providing solutions to wrongdoing acts. Unfortunately they did not support Gotlieb, which also was an important condition in achieving effectiveness of the whistle-blowing according to Near and Miceli, (1995). The fact that NZA was both the complaint recipient and the wrongdoer did not support the situation described in the case study.

3) Characteristics of the wrongdoer

Although it is hard to identify individuals who are responsible for the wrongdoing, the size of the wrongdoing act was extensive and should have been recognized and solved by the management. The power and probably also the credibility of the management is relatively high and therefore this could have decreased the effectiveness. The real problem is of course that the dependence upon the wrongdoing was rather high. This led to a situation in which the management, which had a lot of power, chose not to change the problems described in the current case. On the contrary, it chose to get rid of Gotlieb.

Situational factors

1) Characteristics of the wrongdoing

The wrongdoing act mainly exists out of privacy issues such as the clean desk rule, the possibility to check every employee's agenda and the open accessibility to the V- and W-drive. Though these privacy issues may be illegal, this did not encourage the management to do something about it. When looking at the case it may seem strange the management did nothing while privacy is quite a sensitive topic in the Dutch society. The problem is that changing back office systems requires a lot of change in the company.

2) Characteristics of the organization

Low organization power tends to increase the effectiveness of whistle-blowing. Because NZA has a monopoly position as legislator in the healthcare market, the power of the organization is very high. According to this variable it does not seem to be strange that the whistle-blowing was not effective. However, when looking at the supportive climate, the fact that NZA claims to be a learning organization contradicts the fact that the organization did not solve the problems.

Conclusions

According to the information obtained from the application of the effective whistleblowing model on the NZA case, it can be said that there are several factors that could explain what went wrong. The power of the management was high and as they were not supporting Gotlieb this describes the first restriction in the NZA case. A likely reason why they were not supportive could be that the management was wrongdoer and complaint recipient at the same time. More constraints were caused by situational factors; due to the monopoly of NZA in the market it was not likely for the whistleblowing to be effective. Regarding the claim of NZA to be a learning organization, one should expect though, that the willingness of the management to change is high. Nevertheless, when looking at this case, it should be seriously considered if NZA could name itself a learning organization after all.

5.3. Whistleblowing program costs and benefits

In the previous sections the variables in the decision making process whether or not to blow the whistle as well as the prerequisite for a successful whistleblowing program were explained. Now, let's take a look into the motivation for employment of a whistleblowing program. In particular the costs and benefits of employing an effective whistleblowing program will be explained and mapped with the case.

The purpose of a whistleblowing program is to encourage using internal way when communicating a wrongdoing instead of going public. It has to take advantage of the opportunities that whistleblowing offers but without encouraging complaints with no reasonable basis that are pointed at asserting or challenging the authority. (Miceli and Near, 1994)

The benefits and costs will be made apparent using a case from a large hospital. The actual name of the company is disguised for confidentiality. An employee in this hospital found physical evidence for the presence of bacteria in the anesthesia equipment that could cause pneumonia and other diseases. He desperately advised that the equipment should be cleaned after every use, which was not done currently. The management however did not respond to this warning but rather punished the employee, similar to the NZA case. His access to sections of the hospital was restricted and he was reprimanded. He was even asked if he could provide the funds for the cleaning himself. (Miceli and Near, 1994)

Next to the purely human perspective, ethical and legal issues are raised by this incident. Clearly the employee could make this evidence public, which would have huge consequences from the hospital. These will be summarized in categories below.

First of all, there are monetary damages that threaten the hospital. Fines and not to mention law suits, should even one patient get sick due to the neglected maintenance. These costs would far more overweigh the funds needed for a regular maintenance.

Furthermore if an employee gets sick because of contact with the contaminated instruments, the resulted lost sick days cost the hospital as well.

Next to that if the wrongdoing becomes public; the adverse publicity would damage the hospital for a long period of time. Not only would patients stop going there but also cooperation with other hospitals, networks etc. will be damaged.

This could also lead to more inspections and possibly additional legislative actions.

Internally this would affect the culture. Apparently this is a short-sighted approach to management, since it ignores the wrongdoing and this would result in a culture, where wrongdoings are tolerated or encouraged. In this case it is less likely that the hospital will be attractive to specialists as well. This will inevidently lead to less employee loyalty and possibly less specialists working for this hospital. (Miceli and Near, 1994)

If a valid internal whistleblowing program is employed, all of this can be avoided. Furthermore such program can save the company money. An example for this is another large hospital, where an internal auditor discovers that the Director of Pharmacy is stealing drugs and reselling them. By communicating this, he saves the company yearly 300,000$. (Miceli and Near, 1994)

Furthermore the information provided by whistleblowers is mostly useful and it often provides solutions to problems. So, the managers can not only receive information provided directly from employees witnessed the wrongdoing but also proactively make use of the proposed solutions. (Miceli and Near, 1994)

To sum up the benefits associated with employing a valid internal whistleblowing program are monetary, in terms of savings and absence of punishment fees and lawsuits, prevent of adverse publicity and employee de-motivation and fluctuation, and a culture, which does not tolerate wrongdoings.

However a whistleblowing program does not come without costs. These costs are much less than the costs that arise from not having one. The costs include costs associated with creating an appropriate culture, setting up internal report mechanisms, codes of ethic and communication policies, creating stimuli for communication of observed wrongdoings etc.

If we would have to apply this to the current situation, the benefits would also be clearly visible. The biggest costs would, although hard to measure, be the reputational damage done to NZA by ignoring Gotlieb. In addition, the family is starting a lawsuit and the Dutch government is also investigating the current situation. Furthermore the management team responsible for the acts already withdrew itself from its position.

The problem was of course that the company was quite dependent on the software system within this case, which led to a culture in which whisteblowing and a form of open communication did not lead to any changes.

One of the possible options to change, and the one that will be discussed in the discussion/recommendations section is the creation of a learning organization. Something that NZA already claimed to be. What kind of influence this would have on the variables described in the models will be explained in this section as well.

6. Conclusion

The revised model of Keil et all. (2010) tells us that trust in supervisor, management responsiveness and organizational climate conduciveness. While it is very difficult to measure the level of influence the variables have when blowing the whistle we can conclude that it is especially management responsivess that played an important role in the current NZA case. Gotlieb tried to convince the senior staff that it had to change the current situation within the company. The staff has been ignoring him for more than 4 years which ultimately led to the current situation.

The trust Gotlieb had in his supervisors diminished as they ignored him. In addition, the bullying, the increased workload and the negative feedback on his job performance did decrease the level of trust as well. Oddly enough, Gotlieb tried to influence the senior staff of the company for a period of 4 years. Somehow, he maintained a certain level of trust which made him believe that one day the management would actually accept the changes proposed.

The personal reporting responsibility Gotlieb had contained the responsibility towards senior officers when discussing the treatment involving costly medicines. Since the drives discussed in the previous parts were used by every employee he witnessed the wrongdoing. This makes him responsible for reporting it to the senior management and therefore increased the benefit to cost differential described in the model.

The senior management involvement is rather high. From the case it seems that the senior staff had the ultimate power to decide whether or not to implement the changes that Gotlieb proposed. The case also shows that the management was actually trying to get rid of Gotlieb by bullying him, giving him negative feedback on his job performance and increasing his workload to 2.0 FTE. It therefore seemed that the senior management involvement is rather high, but in a negative perspective.

The variable unanimity did not play a role in the current case.

The organizational climate and culture was very hard to determine. We only know that NZA claimed to be a learning organization and that it had a monopoly on the market. This might have led to a too-important-to-fail attitude that ultimately led to not listening to Gotlieb.

The effective whiste-blowing model described by Near & Miceli (1995) gives a more interrelated perspective about whisteblowing. It describes both the characteristics of the whiste-blower and the wrongdoer while also taking the situational factors into account.

What we can learn from this current case study is that especially the organization's dependence on the wrongdoing played an important role. The whole organization was dependent on the usage of the different drives. To change the whole system would lead to a rather big change within the company. Although Arthur Gotlieb showed an extreme amount of evidence and while he wanted to protect privacy of the people involved, the willingness to change was still extremely low. The enormous amount of proof and the legal basis concerning the privacy of clients apparently did not convince the senior staff to change the situation.

Al these variables were already proven to be valid and the current case study once again shows the importance of these variables in whistle-blow activities.

The organization itself obviously did not favor whistle-blowing activities. The fact that they have a monopoly and that they are quite bureaucratic supports this fact.

The biggest issue in the personal characteristics of this particular case study is the fact that the management did have a power position. Arthur Gotlieb was dependent upon the management to change the problems he addressed. Not only did the management ignore the problem, it heavily abused its power by bullying Gotlieb and by addressing him a lot of work while ignoring mails.

Apparently Gotlieb did not have enough credibility to convince the management of changing the current behavior.

What has to be taken into account is that the model is not completely valid. Position power, organizational dependence of the wrongdoing and power of the complaint recipient are tested and proven to be valid variables influencing whistle-blow decision making. This is once again confirmed since all these variables do play a really important role in the current case. While we do not want to draw any conclusions, the current case study tells us that especially the power the management had towards Gotlieb played a pivotal role.

This lead to the fact that the wrongdoing was not terminated. While nothing is said about the organization's performance we can conclude that the company no longer had any control about the external environment. At the 10th of January Gotlieb handed in the file and almost two weeks later he committed suicide. At that point of the time, the media caught the news and started to investigate everything. This led to the situations described above.

We can therefore see that the variables already proven valid once again played an important role within the current case study. However, this research also showed some possible recommendations and discussion points when analyzing the case study. This will be discussed in the recommendations/discussion section.

7. Recommendation/Discussion

Within this section I will discuss the outcome of the models and give possible recommendations about how to prevent likewise situations. What once again has to be taken into account is that a case study has a lower generalizability. Although the valid variables proven in the models once again proved to be important, this does not mean that the current recommendations could work for other companies. What can be said is that these variables are validated and therefore do play an important role. Companies therefore should take these into account and implement changes to prevent these situations from happening.

However, what is not explained in the model are the relationships between the variables itself. While the end result of all the variables leads to a cost/benefit differentiation/organizational willingness to change, the variables could also be explaining each other. Something not explained in the models is this interdependence between variables. A good example could be that management responsiveness could very likely influence the trust in the supervisor. Because models might leave certain variables out (unobserved variables), it is very important to check for this interdependence. This might change the causal link in the models described, in which responsiveness of the management leads to either a higher or lower trust in the supervisor ultimately leading to the cost/benefit differential. Therefore the trust in the supervisor is all of a sudden an intermediate variable. This completely changes the current model. It is, therefore, very important in future research to check the interdependence between these variables.

A more ideal organizational format to strive for could be a learning organization. In his book The Fifth Discipline: The Art and Practice of the Learning Organization, Peter Senge identifies five main characteristics important when striving to become a learning organization. These can be seen in figure 5.

Figure 5: Five characteristics of learning organization (Senge, 2006)

Systems thinking

The idea of the learning organization is developed from systems thinking. Organizations are a system of interrelationships. Analyzing these relationships and identifying/filtering the problems within them allows an organization to perform at a higher level. Having information systems in place is important to accomplish this.

Personal mastery

Individual focus on becoming better at your work is a step towards learning, so there is a competitive advantage for an organization whose workforce can learn more quickly than the workforce of other organizations. This can be acquired through staff training and development programs. Learning cannot however be forced upon an individual who is not receptive to learning. Research shows that most learning in the workplace is incidental and not the result of intended (formal) training. Therefore it is important to develop a culture where personal mastery is practiced in daily life. A learning organization has been described as the sum of individual learning, but there must be mechanisms for individual learning to be transferred into organizational learning.

Mental models

The assumptions and believes held by individuals and organizations are called mental models. To become a learning organization, these models must be challenged. Both individuals and organizations have attitudes, norms and values that exist on 'paper' (intended conduct) and attitudes, norms and values that are actually applied to certain situations (theories in use). In creating a learning environment it is important to replace confrontational attitudes with an open culture that promotes inquiry and trust. Unwanted values need to be discarded in a process called unlearning. The three step change model of Lewin that is addressed in the book of John Hayes (The Theory and Practice of Change Management, p.59) can be helpful at this stage. Lewin describes the steps:

- Unfreeze; examine status quo, increase driving forces for change and decrease resisting forces against change.
- Change; take action and make change towards desired level (learning organization).
- Refreeze; establishment of new attitudes, norms and values as the new status quo.

Shared vision

The development of a shared vision is important in motivating employees to learn, because it creates a common identity that provides focus and motivation for learning. The most successful visions build on the individual visions of the employees at all levels of the organization, thus the creation of a shared vision can be hindered by traditional structures where the company vision is imposed from above. Therefore, learning organizations ideally have flat, decentralized organizational structures. This is certainly not the case at NZA, which is a very bureaucratic and hierarchal organization. Next to competitive performance, there should also be long term goals that are intrinsic within the company.

Team learning

As does individual vision builds an organization wide vision, so does the combined learning of individuals within an organization constitutes team learning. The benefit of team or shared learning is that staff grows more quickly and the problem solving capacity of the organization is improved through better access to knowledge and expertise. Openness, engaging in discussion and dialogue and open communication are very important to accomplish this.

With the case in mind, the last three characteristics focus most on creating an open organization (and culture) in which it is not frowned upon to stop and think a 'second' about an organization's conduct. Off course, while in a learning organization a bottom up approach is encouraged, getting the wheels turning requires organizational wide support and a shared goal. A CEO can take the lead in this and communicate to the rest of the organization that for example

- All internal complaints coming directly to them in the first instance.
- Make it clear to subordinates that any victimization of complainants will not be tolerated.
- Follow up outcomes of complaints.

8. References

Blackburn, M. S. (1988). Employee dissent: The choice of voice versus silence. Doctoral dissertation, University of Tennessee Knoxville.

Bowie, N. E. and R. F. Duska: 1990, *Business Ethics*, 2nd ed. (Prentice Hall, Englewood Cliffs New
Jersey).

Brown, A.J. (2008). Whistleblowing in the Australian Public Sector: Enhancing the Theory and Practice of Internal Witness Management in Public Sector Organisations (ANU E Press).

Chambers, A. (1995). 'Whistleblowing and the Internal Auditor', *Business Ethics: A European Review* **4**, 192–198.

Chiasson, M., Johnson, H.G. and Byington, J.R. (1995). 'Blowing the Whistle: Accountants in Industry', *CPA Journal*, February, 24–27.

Conlee, M.C., and Tesser, A. (1973). The Effects of Recipient Desire to Hear on News Transmission. Sociometry *36*, 588.

De Maria, W. (1994). Unshielding the Shadow Culture (Department of Social Work and Social Policy, University of Queensland).

Dohmen, J., & Wester, W. (2014, April 10). Het NZa-dossier: wanorde bij de toezichthouder. *NRC Next.*

Dozier, J.B., and Miceli, M.P. (1985). Potential Predictors of Whistle-Blowing: A Prosocial Behavior Perspective. Acad. Manage Rev. *10*, 823.

Gerring, J. (2004). What Is a Case Study and What Is It Good for? American Political Science Review, 341-354.

Gerring, J. (2012). Social science methodology: a unified framework. *Strategies*

Gundlach, M.J., Douglas, S.C., and Martinko, M.J. (2003). The Decision to Blow the Whistle: A Social Information Processing Framework. Acad. Manage. Rev. *28*, 107–123.

Hayes, J. (2014). The Theory and Practice of Change Management. *New York: Palgrave Macmillan.* 4rd Edition.

Hirschman, A. O. (1970). Exit, Voice and Loyalty: Responses to Decline in Firms, Organisations and States. *Harvard University Press, Cambridge Mass.*

Jubb, P.B. (1999). Whistleblowing: A Restrictive Definition and Interpretation. *Journal of Business Ethics* 21: 77–94.

Keil, M., Smith, H.J., Pawlowski, S., and Jin, L. (2004). "Why didn"t somebody tell me?': climate, information asymmetry, and bad news about troubled projects. ACM SIGMIS Database *35*, 65–84.

Keil, M., Tiwana, A., Sainsbury, R., and Sneha, S. (2010). Toward a Theory of Whistleblowing Intentions: A Benefit-to-Cost Differential Perspective*. Decis. Sci. *41*, 787–812. Lennane, J. (2012). What Happens to Whistleblowers, and Why. *Social medicine.* Volume 6, Number 4, p.249-258.

Miceli, M.P., and Near, J.P. (2002). What Makes Whistle-Blowers Effective? Three Field Studies. Hum. Relat. *55*, 455–479.

Miceli, M.P., and Near, J.P. (1994). Whistleblowing: Reaping the benefits. Acad. Manag. Exec. *8*, 65–72.

Miceli, M. P. and Near, J.P. (1992). Blowing the Whistle. (Lexington Books, New York).

Miceli, M.P., and Near, J.P. (1984). The Relationships Among Beliefs, Organizational Position, and Whistle-Blowing Status: A Discriminant Analysis. Acad. Manage. J. *27*, 687–705.

Morrison, E.W., and Milliken, F.J. (2000). Organizational Silence: A Barrier to Change and Development in a Pluralistic World. Acad. Manage. Rev. *25*, 706.

Near, J. P., & Miceli, M. P. (1995). Effective-Whistle Blowing. Academy of Management Review, 20(3), 679–708. doi:10.5465/AMR.1995.9508080334

Senge, P. M., & Suzuki, J. (1994). *The fifth discipline: The art and practice of the learning organization* (p. 14). New York: Currency Doubleday

Smith, H.J., Keil, M., and Depledge, G. (2001). Keeping mum as the project goes under: Toward an explanatory model. J. Manag. Inf. Syst. *18*, 189–228.

Soeken, K.L. and Soeken, D.R. (1987). A Survey of Whistleblowers: Their Stressor and Coping Strategies. University of Maryland. p. 1-17.

9. Appendix

Summary 1

Whistleblowing: Reaping the benefits
M. Miceli and J. Near (1994)

Whistleblowing cases followed by no changes in the organization and "terrible experience" of the whistleblower are not rare anymore. Only few enterprises have established innovative programs to encourage valid internal Whistleblowing. The emphasis here should be on internal and valid. An effective internal Whistleblowing program could prevent external Whistleblowing to a large extend. Encouraging only valid Whistleblowing would avert threats for filing complaints just to assert or challenge authority. The absence of such program and/or lack in its effectiveness can lead to reputational losses, profitability decline, and employees' demoralization and could result in fines or a costly lawsuit.

- Hospital case – bacteria causing pneumonia and other diseases grows in anesthesia equipment not being cleaned after every use. Even though the employee brought up physical evidence, no changes were made. (he was asked if he personally could provide the funds for cleaning, as "times were tough" at the hospital). As a result: the employee was mistreated and his access to sections in the hospital – restricted.
- Ethical and legal concerns
- Short-sighted approach to management, ignoring the wrongdoing
- Losing a lawsuit would overweight the costs of regular cleaning and maintenance
- Employees also at risk, so lost sick days
- Whistleblowing program does not come without cost but its cost are much less than the costs that arise from not having one
- Monetary damages, adverse publicity, increased level of inspections and even additional legislative actions, effects on culture (becoming one that encourages wrongdoing) and therefore on quality of workforce
- Move away from the "doing nothing" managerial approach to proactive creation of climate for correcting wrongdoing
- Need for communicating policies and codes of ethics – statement of what is considered to be wrong; what actions are desired, who to inform etc
- Encouraging internal Whistleblowing – example: internal auditor at a large hospital discovered that the Director of Pharmacy is engaged in stealing drugs from the hospital and reselling them. This saved the company 300.00 $ a year
- Responsiveness of complaints – employees are not always required by law to use internal channels first before making the claim public
- If claim against direct supervisor, need for another internal channels even anonym arises, such as trainer or internal organizational development consultant
- Utilizing alternative reporting mechanisms – anonymous suggestions, such as the "open door" policy at IBM and the "Open Line" program of Bank of America; arbitration, such as the American Arbitration Association –cost per case between 200 $ and 1500 $, two to three months for resolution; in-house review panel (peer-review panel with five individuals, 2 managers and 3 employees)

- For a whistleblower willingness to correct wrongdoing is even higher stimulus for internal Whistleblowing than cash rewards or letters of commendation

Summary 2

Toward a theory of Whistleblowing Intentions: A Benefit-to-Cost Differential Perspective
M. Keil, A. Tiwana, R. Sainsbury, S. Sneha (2010)

Different factors that could influence Whistleblowing intentions are mentioned in the dominant research however with no assessment of the way of their influence. Therefore a middle-range theory of Whistleblowing is developed and tested by Keil et al that explains how and why a variety of factors may influence Whistleblowing intentions. The central premise is that a perceived "benefit-to-cost differential" mediates the relationship between Whistleblowing factors and Whistleblowing intentions. The "benefit-to-cost differential" is the central explanatory variable. It is the net difference between the perceived costs and the expected benefits of Whistleblowing, as perceived by a potential whistleblower. (Keil et al, 2010). It is claimed that individuals weigh the relative costs and benefits and this leads to their decision whether or not to blow the whistle.

- However focus of the article on Whistleblowing intensions of IT project managers, so questionable/ limited generalizability.
- Analysis of the extent to which IT project managers weigh the costs and benefits of Whistleblowing in their evaluation of the factors believed to influence Whistleblowing intensions
- Even noticing failure of a project coming up, they may choose not communicate this higher in the hierarchy.
- Fear of reprisal that includes harassment, slander, reprimands, punitive transfers, threats, demotion and dismissal
- The "mum effect" – natural human reluctance to transmit bad news and unwillingness to bear the cost associated the transmission of bad news (Tesser and Rosen, 1975), such as the fear of negative evaluation. (in the 70ties)
- "Whistleblowing" (in the 80ties)
- Dozier and Miceli (1985) model of some factors that influence the Whistleblowing process
- Micheli and Near (1992) state that the decision whether or not to blow the whistle depends on the presence (or absence) of available alternatives and whether the benefits associated with blowing the whistle will outweigh the costs
- Micheli and Near (1985) – a factor is to which extent whistleblowers can benefit in case a corrective action is taken. Intrinsic rewards (improvement of working life etc) and direct rewards (cash rewards etc) are also proposed
- Next to the fore mentioned costs in regard to fear of reprisal, Micheli and Near (1992) propose also the costs of "risk of feared consequences".
- The concept of "organizational silence", when employees know the truth about wrongdoings but do not communicate this (Morrison & Milliken, 2000) linked to organizational culture

- Selection of factors based on the social information processing framework of Whistleblowing by Gundlach, Douglas and Martinko (2003) – review of the Whistleblowing literature
- Factors to positively influence the decision to blow the whistle – personal reporting responsibility (supported), trust in supervisor (s), reporting anonymity (s), management responsiveness (s) and organizational climate conduciveness (s)
- Negative influence on intention to blow the whistle – ability to hide information, senior management attachment to project (both hypothesis not supported)
- From the resulting benefit-to-cost differential associated with reporting bad news and its influence on the Whistleblowing intention
- Revised model: two of the Whistleblowing factors (personal responsibility and reporting anonymity) exert their influence on Whistleblowing intentions solely through the perceived benefit-to-cost differential. Three other factors (trust in supervisor, management responsiveness and organizational climate conduciveness) are partially mediated by the perceived benefit-to-cost differential. The influence of many factors is mediated by the benefit-to-cost differential and therefore its importance.
- The key for an organization is to keep the benefit-to-cost differential as high as possible for the individual by maximizing the benefits of reporting (Whistleblowing) and/or minimizing the costs.

Summary 3

"Effective whistleblowing"
Near, J.P & Miceli, M.P (1995)

Although whistleblowing could lead to positive change it must be handled effectively to do so. Effective whistleblowing is defined as "the extent to which the questionable or wrongful practice (or omission) is terminated at least partly because of whistleblowing and within a reasonable time frame". Both potential whistle-blowers and managers do not benefit by ineffective whistleblowing. The purpose of this article is to determine predictors that increase the likelihood of effective whistle-blowing by presenting a model and propositions which are derived from this model. In the model five factors are shown which could influence the 'termination of wrongdoing'. The termination of wrongdoing could affect both the organizations' future performance and the organizations' control of elements in the external environment.

FIGURE 1
Individual Variables That Affect the Outcome of Whistle-blowing

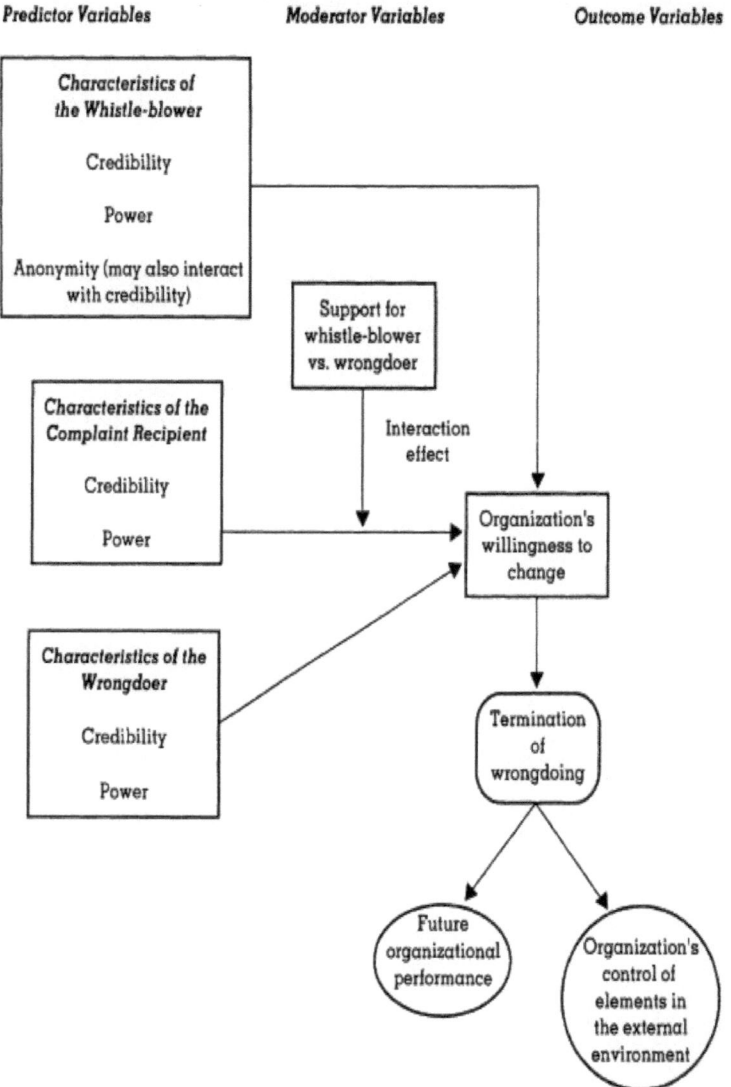

FIGURE 2
Situational Variables That Affect the Outcome of Whistle-blowing

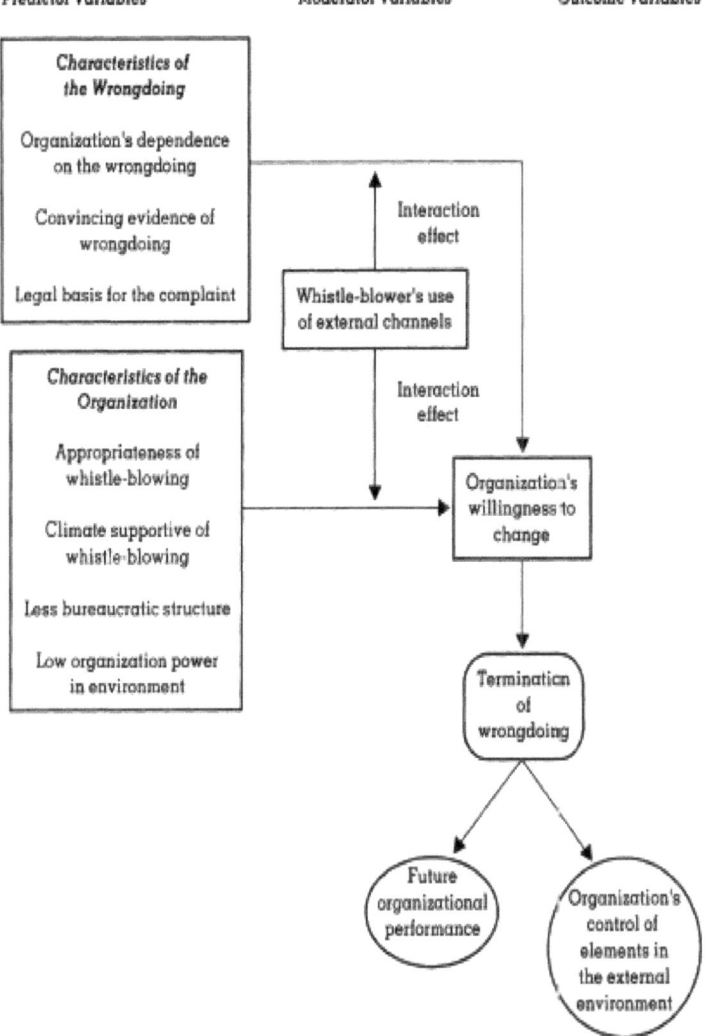

Theoretical framework of the model

Whistleblowing can be seen as an 'influence process' which means that a whistleblower tries to change the behavior of an organization by terminating their wrongdoing. The authors explain the process by using both change as power theories. Power theories focus on the extent to which a whistleblower has the possibility to create organizational change due to their power they have in an organization. It is possible to examine four perspectives on power: 1) resource dependence, 2) value congruence, 3) minority influence in groups, and 5) individual power bases.

Propositions based on the model

The authors are suggesting that several variables influence the efectiveness of whistle-blowing.

Characteristics of the whistleblower

Credibility: If a whistleblower has credibility it is more likely for him to reach and convince the management of their wrongdoing. Credibility depends on perceived motives of whistleblowers. Factors that increase the credibility will probably lead to a higher level of efectiveness.

Power: Organizational status can be seen as power and reflects the way in which an organization depends on the whistle-blower. Power can be measured by different factors: Education level, tenure, support from superiors, lack of retaliation when the whistle-blowing occurs, position in the hierarchy, pay grade, professional status and membership in a majority group.

Anonymity of the whistle-blower: Efectiveness will increase when a whistle-blower identifies himselve instead of stayin anonimous, unless doing so would reduce credibility.

Characteristics of the complaint recipient

Complaint recipients have to determine a) whether the wrongdoing has occurred, b) whether they are responsible and c) whether they have the power to change the wrongdoing. The complaint recipients are often guided by the ethical climate of the organization. Effectiveness will be enhanced when complaint recipients are credible and powerful, but only if they are also supportive of the whistle-blower.

Characteristics of the wrongdoer

Power of wrongdoers influences the way in which the organization protects them. Credibility may be related to power, but credible wrongdoers may nog have much power. Effectiveness will increase when the wrongdoer has little power and/or credibility

Characteristics of the wrongdoing

Dependence on wrongdoing: Risk of the wrongdoing may be balanced against the costs of change. The greater the dependence of the organization on the wrongdoing, the less the effectiveness and the more likely that external whistle-blowing will be effective.

Convincing evidence of wrongdoing: Effectiveness increases when evidence that the wrongdoing has occurred is convincing.

The legal basis for the complaint: Effectiveness will increase when whistle-blowers report activity that is clearly illegal and unambiguous.

Characteristics of the organization

Appropriateness of whistle-blowing: Effectiveness will be affected by the perceptions of coworkers, management, and the complaint recipient concerning the extent to which the whistle-blower's reporting the particular incident in question is prescribed as appropriate by the organization of by informal norms.

Organizational climate: Effectiveness increases in organizations in which the climate discourages wrongdoing, encourages whistle-blowing, and discourages retaliation against whistle-blowers.

Organization structure: Effectiveness will be enhanced in organizations with bureaucratic structures, but only if formal mechanisms exist to encourage internal whistle-blowing and if they actually operate consistent with the formalization

Power of the organization: Effectiveness will increase in organizations that have low power in their environments, especially if external channels of reporting are used

Conclusions

Proponents of prescriptive models argue that whistle-blowing improves organizational innovation or ethical decision making in organizations and therefore whistle-blowing should increase. Whistleblowing is often ineffective and benefits no-one. Future research should focus on identifying the conditions under which whistle-blowing can be effective. Organizations that are truly committed to the goals of avoiding and correcting wrongdoing would be very interested in maintaining conditions that will support change efforts without disrupting the smooth functioning of their operations. Propositions in this report are a starting point to validate recommendations which are often made to whistle-blowers about how to enhance their efficacy and to explain to managers how they can respond in the best way to whistle-blowing.

Summary 4

The decision to blow the whistle: A social information processing framework.
Gundlack, M.J., Douglas, S.C. & Martinko, M.J. (2003)

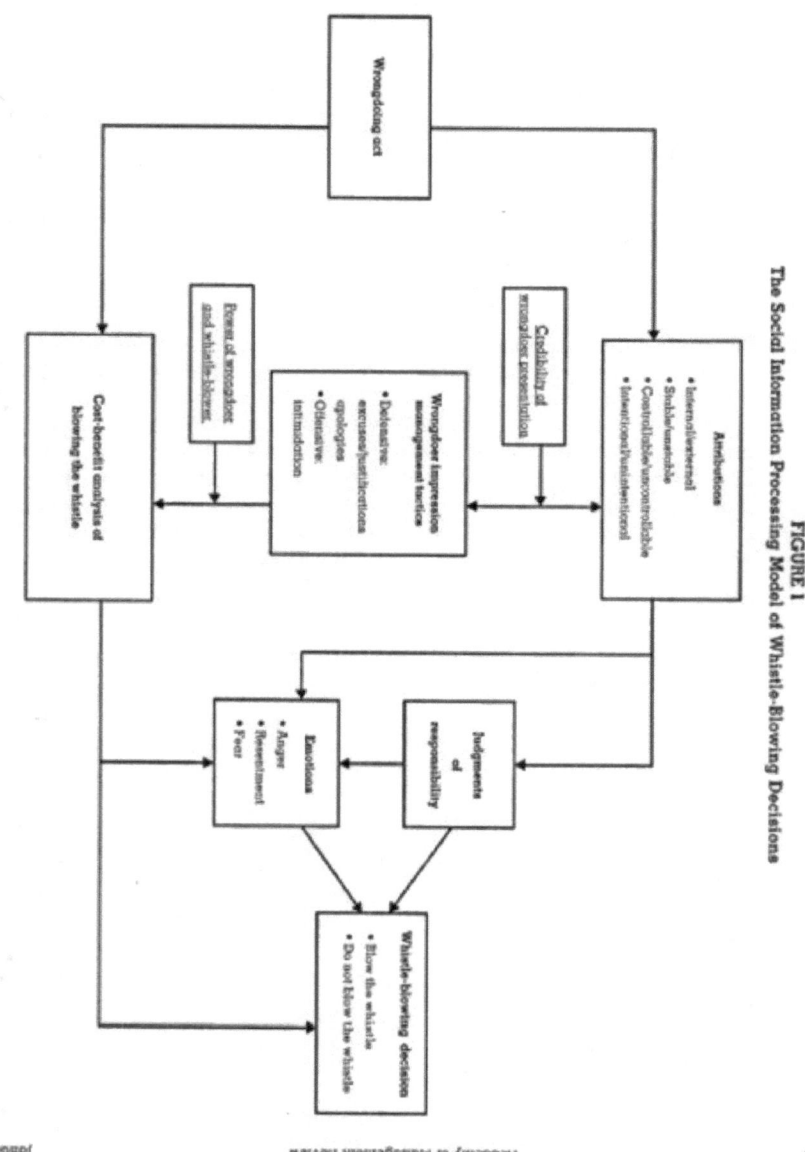

The article shows a social information processing model based on the integration of power, justice and prosocial theories. Model illustrates the influence of attributions and responsibility judgments of individuals and their cost-benefit analysis of the wrongdoing on their emotions and decisions to blow the whistle. The framework illustrates how whistle-blowing decisions evolve at both the inter- as intrapersonal level. Additionally the researchers demonstrate how wrongdoers can use impression management tactics to manipulate whistle-blowing decisions.

Intrapersonal factors

Attributions, judgments of responsibility, and emotions:

Proposition 1a: To the extent potential whistle-blowers attribute acts of perceived wrongdoing to internal, stable, and controllable causes, they will hold wrongdoers responsible.

Proposition 1b: To the extent potential whistle-blowers hold wrongdoers responsible, they will decide to blow the whistle.

Proposition 2a: To the extent potential whistle-blowers attribute acts of perceived wrongdoing to internal stable, controllable, and intentional causes, they will experience anger and resentment toward the perceived wrongdoers.

Proposition 2b: To the extent potential whistleblowers hold wrongdoers responsible, they will experience the emotions and anger and resentment toward the perceived wrongdoers.

Proposition 2c: To the extent potential whistle-blowers experience the emotions of anger and resentment toward the perceived wrongdoers, they will decide to blow the whistle.

Cost-benefit analysis: Whistle-blowers consider the economic and psychological costs and benefits of their reporting.

Proposition 3: To the extent potential whistle-blowers believe the benefits of whistle-blowing outweigh the costs, they will decide to blow the whistle.

Interpersonal factors

Focus in this section lies on how wrongdoers can use social influence through impression management tactics to manipulate whistle-blowing decisions.

Defensive impression management:

Proposition 4: Wrongdoers' excuses and justifications for perceived wrongdoing increase the probability that potential whistle-blowers will make uncontrollable and unstable attributions for wrongdoing behavior.

Proposition 5: Wrongdoer apologies increase the probability that potential whistle-blowers will make unstable attributions for wrongdoing behavior.

Offensive impression management: Tactics such as intimidation (threats or retaliation) are used by wrongdoers; this may result in either fear which decreases the intention to blow the whistle, or anger/resentment which motivates the whistle-blower.

Proposition 6: a) Wrongdoer intimidation increases the probability that potential whistle-blowers will make internal, controllable, stable, and intentional attributions that will increase judgments of wrongdoer responsibility, b) increases perceived costs of blowing the whistle and c) if fear is bigger than anger/resentment whistle-blower will decide to not blow the whistle.

Moderators

Credibility and Power:

Proposition 7: Likelihood that a wrongdoer excuses, justifications or apologies, result in attributional patterns that, in turn, reduce perceptions of responsibility and lessen emotions of anger and resentment toward wrongdoers will be stronger to the extent they are perceived to be credible.

Proposition 8: Likelihood that wrongdoer intimidation results in cost-benefit analysis that induce fear will be stronger to the extent potential whistle-blowers believe wrongdoers have more power.

Summary 5

Whistleblowing: A Restrictive Definition and Interpretation
Jubb, P.B. (1999)

Whistleblowing has been defined often and in differing ways in the literature. Jubb tries to clarify the meaning of whistleblowing and to speak for a narrow interpretation of it. A restrictive, general purpose definition is provided which contains six necessary elements:

- act of disclosure
- actor
- disclosure subject
- target
- disclosure recipient
- outcome

Whistleblowing is characterised as a dissenting act of public accusation against an organisation which necessitates being disloyal to that organisation.

There are three major goals a whistleblower can have, these are:

- Informing; the release of information is done deliberately and with the aim of achieving a disclosure.
- Accusation; identifies perceived wrongdoing, typically a bad news message about misconduct, incompetence, fraud, etc. alleged to have been ignored and/or covered up. In any case an accusation is being made towards some person or organization.
- Dissent (disagreement); when faced with wrongdoing, a person can choose to disagree with the observed misconduct. During this there are three options which are mentioned in the paragraph below.

	Nature of the perceived activity triggering the concern			
	Illegal, immoral or illegitimate		Not illegal immoral or illegitimate	
	Exit dimension			
Expression of the concern (voice)	Stay	Go	Stay	Go
External dissent to someone who can take action	External whistle-blowing	Exit with public protest[b]	Secret sharing	Exit with secret sharing
Internal dissent to someone who can take action	Internal whistle-blowing	Protest during exit interview[b]	Employee participation, grievance	Explain reason for resignation in exit
Dissent in some other form	Discussion, confrontation with wrongdoer	Exit with notice to wrongdoer	Sabotage, strikes	Sabotage, strikes with exit
No expressed dissent	Inactive observation[c]	Inactive departure	Silent disgruntlement	Silent departure

The distinction between internal and external whistleblowing and the decision whether to include both in a definition open to discussion/interpretation. For example, it is "not claimed that the disclosure must be made known to the general but it does mean that the whistleblower's information is accessible without too many bureaucratic obstacles."

The author decides on the above mentioned six elements which can be seen in the table below.

The dissection		
Element	Descriptor	Elaboration
1 ACTION	Whistleblowing	
2 OUTCOME	Is a disclosure	. . . deliberate . . . non-obligatory
3 ACTOR	On public record	
4 SUBJECT	By a person with privileged access to an organisation's data or information	. . . present or former
5 TARGET	About illegality or wrongdoing	. . . non-trivial . . . actual, suspect, potential . . . under organisation control
6 RECIPIENT	Which implicates the organisation	
	To an external entity	. . . having potential to remedy the wrong

Summary 6

What happens to whistleblowers, and why
Lennane, J. (2012)

The author uses data from previous surveys that were conducted in the U.S. in 1990 and Australia in 1993. She focuses most on the Australian survey that was conducted by Whistleblowers Australia (WBA). The survey consisted of 35 subjects that had blown the whistle on corruption and/or danger to the public, in a period of less than two years to over twenty years ago. They came from a range of occupations – banking/finance, health, law enforcement, local government, transport, teaching and miscellaneous public service, state and federal.

A quick overview of the consequences the whistleblowers were faced with are:

- 90% lost their jobs or were demoted
- 20% got into difficulties with alcohol
- 20% had a long-term relationship break up
- 20% were threatened with a defamation action
- 6% attempted suicide
- 9% went bankrupt

Organization's response

If a person remains in the job, informal tactics are used almost invariably. In the WBA study, these included:

- isolation – from the usual channels of information and consultation (49%); or maybe physical (23%), for example being put in a room with a desk and chair, no telephone
- removal of normal work (43%)
- abuse and denigration, formal and informal, usually by supervisors, who may also encourage other employees to give the whistleblower a hard time (43%)
- minute scrutiny of timesheets and work records, inspections, adverse reports sought from previous employer (34%)
- demanding or impossible orders (26%)
- referral for psychiatric assessment/treatment (37%, plus an attempt to do so in another 9%)
- repeated threats of disciplinary action (20%)

All subjects had initially addressed a problem internally. In 9% of the cases the complaint did not go further, in 91% of the cases the subjects went complained externally (union, local parliamentarian). If that too failed, 49% went to the media. Distinctive in this is that in 83% of the cases the harassment (victimization) occurred immediately after the first internal complaint. The author states that the occurrence of a powerful response means that corruption includes top management. In general the aims of organizations response are:

1) to isolate the whistleblower by removal from the accepted "in-group" (one of us) to "out-group" status, by representing the whistleblower as:
   • incompetent
   • disloyal
   • a ratbag
   • mentally unbalanced/ill

2) to frighten others who might otherwise support the whistleblower.

3) to avoid examining or remedying the issue the whistleblower is complaining about.

Next to this, the wrongdoing continued (71%) and sometimes the wrongdoers were even promoted (26%).

Authorities to which a whistleblowers can reasonably expect to turn to had generally been unhelpful. Examples of authorities are Administrative Appeals Tribunal, industrial relations, ombudsmen, Independent Commission Against Corruption.

Colleagues

Support from colleagues is often not to be expected. Sometimes colleagues actively harass or even betray a whistleblower. If they express support to the whistleblower it is often in a situation in which they are alone and unobserved by other employees/top management (e.g. lift). In general colleagues play it safe and don't want to get involved for fear of similar treatment.

False whistleblowing

The possibility that the complaints made by a whistleblowers are false or malicious has to be taken into account. In general, what counts in the end is that even if whistleblowers were in fact all publicity-seeking ratbags or criminals, examining their sanity, personality, motives and morals is always irrelevant. What matters is whether what they are saying is true.

Obedience to authority

Basic problem that society often faces is that: *that obedience to authority, a basic necessity for constructing and maintaining our society, becomes a powerfully destructive force when that authority is doing wrong.* A study by Stanley Milgram (1974) concluded that people in a situation where they are being told what to do by someone identified as an authority enter a state where they put aside issues of individual responsibility and morality.

Group behavior

Relevant to whistleblowing is the "groupthink" described by Janis (1972) when a cohesive group, often with a dynamic and influential leader, manages to insulate itself from the reality of a situation by ignoring important aspects of it, excluding any member who questions the validity of its decisions. Top management is often in a state of groupthink. The typical whistleblower accumulates a mass of significant documentary evidence and has no difficulty convincing journalists and others outside the organization of the truth of what they are saying. The bureaucracy, however, remains completely convinced that X is a troublemaker whom no one would listen to.

Advice to whistleblowers

20% of the respondents says don't blow the whistle. If you do be very well prepared (document everything, learn legal aspects, trust very few people, try to remain anonymous, get outside help. With regard to that last point it can be said that when whistleblowers consider making a complaint, internal or external, to line up support for themselves before they start. The most reliable support will come from outside the organization – support from within is likely to give once a typical employer reaction starts.

Advice to management

It is not only unethical to support and conceal corruption, it is also bad for business. It is not only unethical to put employees through the prolonged and devastating torment whistleblowers suffer, it will also mean an unhappy, guilty, fearful and much less efficient and productive workforce – bad for business again. Ideally honest CEO's would make sure that the organization is made aware of the following points:

- All internal complaints coming directly to them in the first instance.
- make it clear to subordinates that any victimization of complainants will not be tolerated.

In the end, it comes back to ethics, in management and in the general workforce. An acceptance that corruption, financial or otherwise, is damaging both to the organization and to the whole community, and that whistleblowers represent an important and valuable resource in helping to keep standards the way we would like them to be.

Summary 7

Whistleblowing in organization: An examination of correlates of whistleblowing intentions, actions, and retaliation
Mesmer-Magnus, J. R., & Viswesvaran, C. (2005).

Whistleblowing is "the disclosure by organization members of illegal, immoral or illegitimate practices under the control of their employers, to persons or organizations that may be able to affect action (Mesmer-Magnus and Visweswaran, 2005). Even though whistleblowing via internal channels is less threatening to an organization in comparison with external whistleblowing, the "whistleblower" himself is not often welcomed. This article shows why whistleblowers, even when there is a possibility of retaliation still decide to blow the actual whistle.

The research comprises a Meta-analytic examination of 18.781 persons. The actual goal of the research is to determine what aspects of persons, the context that they live in lead to possible whistelblowing intensions. In addition, do these variables have the same level of influence when the actual whistle has been blown. The authors make this difference to get a greater understanding about the relationship between whistleblowing intent and whistleblowing action. Three different characteristics are described: Whistleblower characteristics, contextual variables and the characteristics of the wrong-doing.

Whistleblower characteristics

The average whistleblower tends to have a good job performance, to be more highly educated, to hold higer-level or supervisory psotions and scores higher on test of moral reasoning. Social-Psychological theories explain that because whistleblowers have a good job performance, they often get some level of lattitude because of their good job performance. Within the research, several demographic characteristics are examined. Results show that the whistleblower age and the level of the job held by the intented whistleblower might best predict whistleblowing intent. Actual whistleblowing is to be predicted by jow level, organiational tenure and seks of the whistleblower.

Contextual variables.

This group of variables explains more variance in an individual's decision to blow the whistle. Contextual variables may include supervisor and coworker support, organizational climate, threat of retaliation and the actual size of the organization. The results show that the organizational climate is indeed positively related to whistleblowing intent. However, this relation is extremely weakened once we discuss whisteblowing action. In addition, retaliation reduces the intented behaviour to blow the whistle, but does not weaken the relationship when discussing actual whisteblowing. Apparently, once the intention is made, retaliation does no longer help.

Characteristics of the wrong-doing.

Empirical research suggest that the perceived severity of the wrongdoing, the evidence of wroingdoing and the characteristics (read: relationship with the whistleblower) of the wrongdoer has significant implications in the decision to blow the whistle. The result led to two interesting conclusions: There was strong correlation between the whistleblowing intent and relational closeness. Secondly, only three percent of the variance in whistleblowing intent and action is explained by severity. Apparently, severe organizational wrongdoing leads to higher retaliation.

Summary 8

Whistleblowing procedures at work: what are the implications for human resource practitioners?
Lewis, D. (2002).

Employees are quite often the first persons that realize that something is going wrong within the company or organization that they work in. However, due to the organizational culture, fear of retaliation and the fear of being disloyal to colleagues makese employees not express their worries. How can a company prevent these problems and thereby avoid possible pitfalls?

First of all a company should formulate a whistleblowing policy. Within this policy a company should state first of all that it takes possible malpractice very seriously and also describe possible malpractices. One of the biggest problems when creating a whistleblowing policy is defining its scope. A good whistblowing programs shows to who it applies and what issues are actually covered. An important feature of this latter point is that the whisteblowing program should not be an extension to or part of an excisting procedure. In addition, procedures about handling grievances or equal opportunity matters should fall outside a whistleblowing procedure.

Secondly, the whisteblowing program should have respect for confidentiality of employees that show their concerns. Companies should try to protect the identity of those that raise an actual concern and do not want their name to be disclosed. On the other side, once an actual investigation is started people have to realize that the source of information is being revealed.

Nevertheless, an organization should reserve the right for people to report wrongdoings in confidence. This confidentiality right should be determined when taking into account factors such as the seriousness of the issues raised and the likelihood of obtaining information from attributable sources.

Thirdly, penalties should be created to prevent possible fals and malicious allegations. Disciplinary rules should show that possible victimisation or deterrment of employees that raise serious concerns constitutes serious misconduct.

In addition, employers should make sure that they clearly show that they will protect themselves and their staff from false statements and malicious expressions.

Fourth, companies should try to create external whisteblow possibilities. It should be stated that the previous points create a situation which specifically encourages workers to seek advice at an early stage. It should show how people can internally blow the whistle and which department has a responsibility.

However, in certain situations some workers might prefer a more objective and independent voice. In addition, employees might be sensible to inform staff about misconduct in the company. It might therefore be sensible to create a external source. Besides this, employees should be informed about the fact that they can be represented by trade unions.

Normally these concerns should be raised at the appropriate level. This is often the immediate supervisor of the employee. However, the most appropriate person to contact will ofcourse depend on the severity and gravity of the misconduct.

Therefore, it is advised that besides the direct supervisor of the employee, other designated persons can be considered contacts if the severity and gravity of the misconduct is so that workers do not want to contact their immediate supervisor.

Last but not least, the possibility to raise a concern should give people the choice to it either verbally or in writing. Ideally, the actual format should be determined in cooperation with trade unions.

Appendix A. Social processing model of whistle-blowing decisions

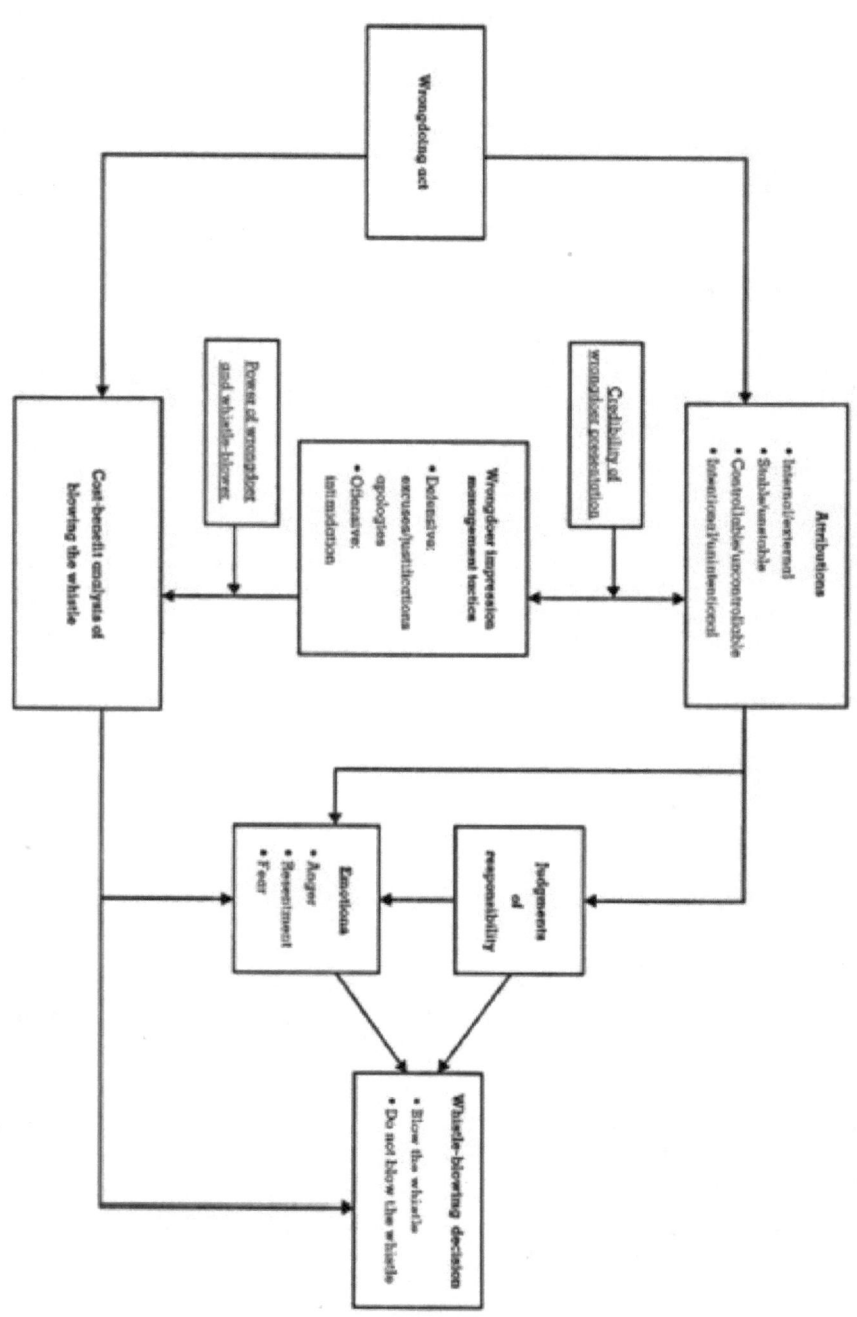